UCHIC

RESEARCH REPORT DECEMBER 2019

English Learners in Chicago Public Schools

A New Perspective

Marisa de la Torre, Alyssa Blanchard, Elaine M. Allensworth, and Silvana Freire

TABLE OF CONTENTS

ACKNOWLEDGEMENTS

The authors wish to acknowledge the educators, school staff, and family members who support English Learners in Chicago Public Schools. We would also like to acknowledge the Chicago Public Schools for their commitment to using research evidence in their ceaseless efforts to improve educational experiences and outcomes of students. The Latino Policy Forum (LPF) has been our partner in this work, and we are so thankful for the contributions of LPF staff on the report, communications strategies, and the advisory committee that they organized and convened. We benefited from the expertise of Sylvia Puente and Karen Garibay-Mulattieri, who provided helpful feedback at all stages of the project. In particular, we would like to thank Rebecca Vonderlack-Navarro, who has been a tireless champion of this project at every stage, organizing our advisory committee, connecting us with experts on Chicago English Learners, and offering extensive written feedback on the report itself.

Prior to writing this report, we presented preliminary findings to the members of our Steering Committee and to the advisory committee convened by LPF. The advisory committee included Samuel Aguirre, Cornelia Grumman, Luisiana Melendez, Elliot Regenstein, Irma Snopek, Sonia Soltero, Robin Steans, and Josie Yanguas, as well as CPS staff members: Anna Szuber, Jorge Macias, Javier Arriola-Lopez, Zhengyun Li, Ryan Marron, and Hilda Cruz-Pena; and representatives from LPF: Erika Mendez, Karen Garibay-Mulattieri, Rebecca Vonderlack-Navarro, Jose Marco-Paredes, and Sylvia Puente. At each presentation, participants asked thought-provoking questions and offered helpful suggestions for our analysis, interpretation, and subsequent writing. Additionally, we received extensive written feedback on the final draft from Steering Committee members Brenda Dixon, Shazia Miller, and Rebecca Vonderlack-Navarro, and thank them for their thorough and

thoughtful comments. The authors thank Jenny Li, Anna Szuber, and Sam Aguirre for their extensive help in understanding state and district policy that governs English Learners. Additionally, we are grateful to Jared Sell, whose help in answering data questions and setting up meetings with district staff was instrumental to our work.

We appreciate the contributions of our Consortium colleagues who read multiple drafts of this report and provided us with valuable suggestions for improvement, including Vanessa Gutiérrez, Jenny Nagaoka, Lisa Sall, Penny Sebring, and Jessica Tansey. We also thank our colleagues Jasmin Lee and Alicia Chen, who conducted a thorough technical read of the report. In addition, the UChicago Consortium's communications team, including Lisa Sall, Jessica Tansey, Jessica Puller, and Alida Mitau, were instrumental in the production of this report. We also appreciate the help of Consortium research assistants Grace Su and Paloma Blandon, who provided background research on the history of English Learners in Chicago and undertook edits of the report. We are grateful for funding from the Spencer Foundation that made this work possible. The UChicago Consortium greatly appreciates support from the Consortium Investor Council that funds critical work beyond the initial research: putting the research to work, refreshing the data archive, seeding new studies, and replicating previous studies. Members include: Brinson Family Foundation, CME Group Foundation, Crown Family Philanthropies, Lloyd A. Fry Foundation, Joyce Foundation, Lewis-Sebring Family Foundation, McCormick Foundation, McDougal Family Foundation, Osa Family Foundation, Polk Bros. Foundation, Spencer Foundation, Steans Family Foundation, and The Chicago Public Education Fund. We also extend our thanks for the operating grants provided by the Spencer Foundation and the Lewis-Sebring Family Foundation, which support the work of the UChicago Consortium.

Cite as: de la Torre, M., Blanchard, A., Allensworth, E.M., & Freire, S. (2019). *English Learners in CPS: A new perspective.* Chicago, IL: University of Chicago Consortium on School Research.

This report was produced by the UChicago Consortium's publications and communications staff: Lisa Sall, Director of Outreach and Communication; Jessica Tansey, Communications Manager; Jessica Puller, Communications Specialist; and Alida Mitau, Development and Communications Coordinator.

Graphic Design: Jeff Hall Design
Photography: Eileen Ryan
Editing: Alida Mitau, Jessica Tansey, and Jessica Puller

10.2019/PDF/jh.design@rcn.com

Executive Summary

In 2018, one-third of students in Chicago Public Schools (CPS) had been classified as English Learners (ELs) at some point in their academic careers.[1]

The district has the responsibility of meeting the educational needs of every student it serves, and understanding the unique needs of ELs is essential, since ELs make up such a large portion of Chicago's students and have the challenge of mastering academic content and learning a new language at the same time. But the statistics normally reported on ELs' academic achievement, and used in school accountability, are based on only a subset of students: those who are "active ELs."[2] Reporting on only this subset of students, and failing to report on all students who entered CPS as ELs, provides a biased picture. Currently, publicly reported data does not allow us to know how all students who began in CPS as ELs, compared to those who did not, are performing academically. There is also little information on how EL students perform on measures of achievement other than test scores.

This study provides new and more nuanced ways of looking at data on ELs' academic performance. We use data from three cohorts of students who were continuously-enrolled in CPS from kindergarten to eighth grade, which includes 18,000 students who began as ELs. We compare students **who began kindergarten as ELs** to students who were **never classified as ELs** to understand their performance and progress over time in school. Then, among students who began kindergarten as ELs, we compare the performance and progress of those **who did** and **who did not reach English proficiency by eighth grade**, in order to understand who may need additional supports, and what those supports may be. For each of these three groups, we examine student performance on a variety of key academic outcomes: attendance, test scores, grades in core subjects, English proficiency, and Freshman OnTrack status for high school graduation.

Key Findings

Students who began school as ELs were different from students never classified as ELs in their backgrounds, but similar in many of their school experiences

Students in our sample who entered kindergarten as ELs were more likely to be economically disadvantaged, as determined by their eligibility for free or reduced-price lunch, and much more likely to be Latino. In Chicago, 90 percent of students who enter kindergarten as ELs are Latino and speak Spanish as their first

---

1 See "Using the Term English Learners" on p.4 for an explanation of why we use this label to describe students whose native language is not English and are working toward developing English proficiency. And see "Glossary" on p.4 for

more detailed definitions of terms used throughout the report.

2 Chicago Public Schools (n.d.), School quality rating policy; Illinois State Board of Education (2018a).

language, while only about 33 percent of the students who are never classified as ELs are Latino. Yet, in many ways the school experiences of ELs in our three cohorts mirrored those of other students. They were just as likely to have attended preschool in CPS as students who were never classified as ELs. They also attended charter schools at similar rates, particularly by the middle grades. While there are concerns about over- or under-classification of ELs as requiring special education services (eligible for an Individualized Education Program), students who began school as ELs in CPS were no more likely to receive special education services as their peers who were never classified as EL in each of the elementary grades.

Publicly-reported statistics often make it look as if EL students are consistently behind non-EL students—but on average, students who began as ELs actually had similar achievement and growth, and higher attendance, compared to students never classified as ELs

A misconception that ELs' academic performance is often below non-ELs' academic performance has stemmed from limitations in publicly available data and reports—namely, the fact that once EL students achieve English proficiency, measured by the ACCESS exam, they are no longer counted in public statistics on ELs' performance, but instead are counted as non-EL students. Thus, public reports that attempt to characterize ELs' academic performance have done so with an incomplete group of students. When we included all students in the CPS cohorts we studied who began kindergarten as ELs, their NWEA-MAP math scores were only slightly lower than those of students never classified as ELs, by about 5 percentile points; and gains on math scores from third to eighth grade were almost identical. In reading, English Learners' third-grade NWEA-MAP scores were lower by about 14 percentile points, which is not surprising, as few students who began as ELs scored above proficiency levels on the ACCESS exam before third grade, and the NWEA-MAP is taken in English. But their growth on reading scores from third to eighth grade was greater than that of other students, so the gap closed by one-half by eighth grade.

Grade point averages (GPAs) were very similar for students who did and did not enter CPS as ELs. One difference was in reading grades from second to sixth grade. Students who entered kindergarten as ELs received lower grades in reading during these years, on average, compared to other students. But by seventh grade, they closed the gap, and there were no differences in students' grades in reading, or in other core classes. When they got to high school, they also had similar Freshman OnTrack rates—a predictor of on-time high school graduation, based on course credits (and failures) —as students who were never classified as ELs.

Students who began as ELs in CPS also had higher attendance rates than students who did not enter kindergarten as ELs. This is especially notable given that EL students were more likely to be economically disadvantaged than other students, and school attendance is influenced by economic factors (for example, having reliable transportation and healthcare).

About one-fifth of students who began as ELs remained classified as ELs upon high school entry

More than one-half of students who began as ELs passed the ACCESS proficiency exam and became former ELs by third grade, and three-fourths passed the exam by the end of fifth grade. If students did not pass the exam by the end of fifth grade, they were unlikely to pass it in the remaining years before high school. This was a large group of students who were continuously labeled as not proficient in English, even though they were continuously enrolled in school. They did not differ from other EL students in the types of schools in which they enrolled (e.g., charter schools, preschools). But they were more likely to be male and were much more likely to be identified as needing special education services than students who reached proficiency on the ACCESS exam before high school.

ELs who did not reach English proficiency before high school had similar growth rates on standardized tests compared to other students

Although about one-fifth of students who began as ELs did not demonstrate proficiency before high school, these students demonstrated growth in their academic skills throughout their K-8 years. Gains on NWEA-MAP reading tests in grades 3-8 were larger for active ELs in eighth grade than those of eighth graders who did reach proficiency and students who were never classified as ELs. They also showed growth on the ACCESS proficiency exam from grades K-3, although they did not reach the benchmark established by the state to demonstrate English proficiency by the end of eighth grade.[3] Notably, students who did not demonstrate proficiency by eighth grade began first grade with scores on the ACCESS that were, on average, lower than those of students who eventually passed the ACCESS exam. Subsequently, because at each grade level students need to get higher scores to demonstrate proficiency on the test, they never scored high enough to meet the proficiency threshold, even though their academic skills increased each year.

ELs who did not reach proficiency before high school were likely to need more support in other areas

Students who did not reach proficiency before high school started out in the primary grades with somewhat higher attendance rates than students who were never classified as ELs, but their attendance declined more in the middle grades than other students. By eighth grade, they had slightly lower attendance than students never classified as ELs. They also had lower Freshman OnTrack rates in the first year of high school than students who demonstrated proficiency by eighth grade, or students never classified as ELs. Their gains on math tests were also slightly lower than those of other students. They did show gains in their course grades from second to eighth grade, but their overall grade point averages were considerably lower than those of students who reached proficiency levels, and students never classified as ELs. Given the large differences in first-grade ACCESS scores between students who reached proficiency before high school and those who did not, it may be possible to identify this group of students early on to provide more support in multiple areas.

Students who demonstrated proficiency by the end of eighth grade had strong academic outcomes

Eighty percent of students who began as ELs demonstrated proficiency on the ACCESS test by the end of eighth grade. They have been categorized in publicly-reported statistics on academic performance as non-ELs once they demonstrated English proficiency, so our analysis of this distinct sub-group of students' academic performance adds a layer of nuance to understanding the full picture of ELs in CPS. Compared to students never classified as ELs, students who began as ELs and demonstrated proficiency by eighth grade had:

- higher attendance through the elementary and middle grades
- higher math NWEA-MAP scores
- higher course grades
- comparable reading NWEA-MAP scores
- comparable Freshman OnTrack rates

In all outcomes, the academic performance of students who began as ELs and demonstrated proficiency by eighth grade was similar to or higher than students who were never classified as ELs, which suggests that students who fall into this category were offered supports appropriate for their academic needs.

Public metrics can give the impression that EL students are lagging behind their peers. However, this new and nuanced look at EL students' academic outcomes shows that, in fact, many EL students made considerable academic progress – on par with or beyond that of their non-EL peers. However, a key group of EL students in our analyses did not reach proficiency by eighth grade; a needs analysis may help to ensure that all students receive the educational supports needed for academic success. Additionally, many questions remain about how EL students perform in different types of schools and programs, their trajectories through high school, and the experiences of students who enter the district as ELs after kindergarten. We hope to address these questions in further studies.

---

3 We examined the ACCESS growth for EL students who did not demonstrate proficiency during the K-3 years because these were the years in which a large group of other EL students with average achievement also took the ACCESS exam, and therefore can serve as a comparison in terms of growth in English proficiency. After third grade, this comparison group of students did not take the ACCESS exam, as they demonstrated proficiency and became former English Learners. Additionally, in these students' later elementary years, the ACCESS test itself changed, making comparisons across years more difficult. Thus, we did not examine ACCESS growth after third grade.

Using the Term English Learners

There is debate about whether the label "English Learners" is the right term to use to describe students whose native language is not English and who are in the process of mastering academic English. Over the past two decades, most states have shifted from the term "limited English proficient" (LEP) to "English language learner" (ELL) to "English Learner" (EL). Publications that focus on this topic also use many other terms, such as "dual language learners," "non-native English speakers," "language-minority students," "bilingual students," or "emerging bilingual students." Some individuals or groups may have strong preferences for one or another. For consistency with what the Illinois state Board of Education stipulates and what CPS uses, the term English Learners (ELs) is used throughout this study.

At the same time, we acknowledge the controversy about the use of the term "English Learner," as it focuses on what students do not know instead of focusing on the strengths, skills, and culture that students bring with them. Educators and policymakers have yet to find a term to identify these students based not only on what they are tasked with learning, but also the rich contributions they make to their school communities. New terms will probably be used in the future, as many districts are recognizing the value being academically proficient in more than one language by awarding the Seal of Biliteracy. The Seal of Biliteracy recognizes students who have studied and attained academic proficiency in two or more languages by high school graduation. From our perspective, the term "English Learner" describes students for whom more is expected than for other students—other students are learning content in their native language (English) while ELs are learning the same content plus a new language.

Glossary

Terms commonly used by federal and state governments to refer to English Learners include:

English Learners (ELs) or Active English Learners: ELs are students "whose home language background is a language other than English and whose proficiency in speaking, reading, writing, or understanding English is not yet sufficient to provide the student with:

1. the ability to meet the State's proficient level of achievement on State assessments;

2. the ability to successfully achieve in classrooms where the language of instruction is English; or
3. the opportunity to participate fully in the school setting." [A]

These students have not yet reached the cut score determined by state on the English proficiency test. This is the group that is usually counted as ELs for reporting purposes in many states.

Former English Learners: Students who were once designated as ELs but demonstrated English proficiency (scored above the cut score) on the English proficiency test and exited out of English Learner status. Usually, these students are not considered in EL performance metrics reports once they have exited their active EL status.

Non-English Learners (Non-ELs): Students who were never classified as ELs or who used to be active ELs — in many reports, former ELs are counted as non-ELs once they have passed the English proficiency test.

In addition to the common terms above, we use the following definitions in this report:

Began as English Learner: Students who were designated as ELs based on the ACCESS[B] test of English proficiency when they entered CPS as kindergartners. This category includes students who later became former ELs or remained as active ELs in their later elementary years.

Demonstrated proficiency by eighth grade: Students who once were ELs but demonstrated proficiency on the ACCESS test before the end of their expected eighth grade year by scoring above the cut point established by the state.

Did not demonstrate proficiency by eighth grade: Students who did not demonstrate English proficiency on the ACCESS test by the end of their expected eighth grade year, given that their scores did not reach the cut point established by the state.

Never classified as EL: Students who were never eligible to receive English Learner services, either because their native language was English or because they took the English proficiency screening test when they began school in CPS and scored high enough on the ACCESS test to be considered proficient in English.

A   Illinois Admin. Code tit. 23, § 228.10 (2017).

B   ACCESS assesses social and academic English proficiency. For more details, see: **https://www.isbe.net/Pages/ACCESS-for-ELLs.aspx**

Introduction

English Learners (ELs)[4] comprise a growing proportion of students in the Chicago Public Schools (CPS) and in schools across the country. While the overall number of students in CPS has been declining, the number of ELs has grown by 32 percent in the last decade. In 2010, ELs represented close to 13 percent of the student population (51,292 students) in the district; in 2019, almost 20 percent of students — a total of 67,664 students—were identified as ELs. Nationally, EL enrollment in public schools has grown by 26 percent from 2000 to 2015, compared with only a seven percent national growth of total student enrollment during the same period.[5]

With the rise in the proportion of ELs in schools across the country comes concerns about whether schools are set up to serve ELs as well as they serve students who begin school already proficient in English. Schools are responsible for making sure students become proficient in English language at the same time they learn the academic content expected for their grade level. But publicly-reported statistics provided by districts and states are not useful for gauging how well ELs are being served. Available public data provide an incomplete, and even misleading, picture of the academic performance of ELs, because they are based on only on active ELs, a subset of the students who begin school as ELs.

These public statistics consistently suggest that ELs are lagging far behind non-ELs academically, which has provoked concerns about how well schools are serving students. For example, results from the English Language Arts (ELA) Partnership for Assessment of Readiness for College and Careers (PARCC) test in Chicago for 2018 showed that 13.2 percent of the ELs in grades 3-8 met or exceeded standards, compared to 31.4 percent of non-ELs. Nationwide, reading data from the National Assessment of Educational Progress (NAEP) test[6] in 2017 showed that there was a 37-point gap between reading scores from non-ELs and ELs in fourth grade, and showed a 43-point gap in eighth grade—a difference roughly comparable to being below the *basic level* vs. below the *proficient level* in this test.[7]

Current reporting on ELs follows the spirit of the No Child Left Behind (NCLB) Act of 2001, which required reporting on subgroups of students by race/ethnicity, free or reduced-price lunch eligibility, whether students had an Individualized Education Program (IEP), and EL status.[8] The impetus behind reporting on these different subgroups was to call attention to groups of students whose academic progress might otherwise have been overlooked if the focus were on overall performance of schools or districts.

---

4   See "Using the Term English Learners" on p.4 for an explanation of why we use this label to describe students whose native language is other than English and are working toward developing English proficiency. And see "Glossary" on p.4 for a more detailed definition of terms used throughout the report.

5   National Center for Education Statistics. (n.d.).

6   The National Assessment of Educational Progress (NAEP) test is administered to a representative sample of fourth, eighth and twelfth graders across the country. NAEP measures what U.S. students know and can do in various subjects (e.g. math, reading, science, U.S. history, civics, geography). Only aggregated results are reported for groups of students with similar characteristics (e.g., gender, race/ethnicity, school location). NAEP achievement levels are reported as Basic, Proficient, and Advanced. For additional information see: https://nces.ed.gov/nationsreportcard/about/

7   National Assessment of Educational Progress. (2017).

8   The IEP is created after a child has been evaluated and found eligible to receive special education and related services.

Different Pictures on EL Performance, Depending on How Students are Grouped

In the 2017-18 school year, 23,414 CPS eighth-graders took the English Language Arts (ELA) PARCC and 24.7 percent of these students met or exceeded expectations. Using PARCC data, we provide an example of how grouping students differently for reporting purposes can give different pictures of how students perform in tests and how schools are serving them. All these different ways of reporting serve specific purposes.

Currently, public reporting focuses on active ELs as a subgroup. These are students classified as ELs because they have not passed the proficiency score on the language proficiency exam (ACCESS). These statistics may be useful to teachers and practitioners to support the students who are working toward acquiring English proficiency. In CPS, there were 2,448 eighth-graders classified as ELs who took the ELA PARCC exam; 1.3 percent of those students met expectations.[C] One could conclude from these numbers that ELs were not being served well, since the performance gap compared to their non-EL peers was large; 27.5 percent of non-ELs met expectations on the exam (see the left panel of Figure A).

However, more than one-quarter of the non-ELs were former ELs who had scored high enough on the ACCESS to be designated English proficient. When former ELs are removed from the non-EL group, the ELA PARCC pass rate for students never classified as ELs goes down to 25.9 percent, while 31.5 percent of former ELs did pass the ELA PARCC (see the middle panel of Figure A). Thus, ELs who acquired English language skills and passed the ACCESS had higher pass rates on the ELA PARCC than students who were never classified as ELs.

Former and active EL groups are defined by their achievement on one standardized test, the ACCESS test. Active ELs, defined by low achievement on the ACCESS, tend to have low average achievement on other assessments, and the reverse is true for former ELs—so any resulting metrics about the academic achievement of these two groups together will be biased. Even a school where almost all students reach proficiency can look like it is poorly supporting ELs, if judged only by the success of its current ELs, who may be a very small subset of the students who began as ELs. Reporting active ELs as a subgroup calls attention to the students who are struggling the most with the difficult task of learning a new language and mastering academic content at the same time. However, judging a school by the ELs who need the most support will not give parents or district decisionmakers a good understanding of how EL students actually perform on average.

C   The Partnership for Assessment of Readiness for College and Careers (PARCC) Test measures students' progress towards state standards in English language arts/literacy and mathematics for grades 3-8 and high school. Scores are reported according to five performance levels that describe what a typical student should be able to demonstrate based on the expectations aligned to grade-level standards. Level 1 indicates that the student has not met these expectations, while Level 5 indicates the strongest performance as the student has exceeded the expectations. For additional information see: https://parcc-assessment.org/

Public reporting on active ELs highlights the needs of students who struggle the most to master English and perform successfully in school. However, using statistics on active EL students may lead to perceptions that all ELs are perpetually behind other students, or that EL services are ineffective, when neither may be the case. The group of students considered active ELs changes as students move through school; students who successfully become proficient in English are dropped from the group of students counted in statistics as active ELs. Instead, they are counted as non-EL students upon reaching English proficiency (see Figure A). Thus, a school could successfully educate ELs so that they have strong academic gains and quickly pass the proficiency test, but those students' achievement would not be included in the school's statistics on active ELs, so parents and district leaders might not know that the school was serving ELs well. Furthermore, the active EL group in any one year is a mix of students who have been receiving English language supports since kindergarten or before, along with new students arriving to the district who may or may not have been learning English before they arrived at the school. It is just not possible to know how ELs are performing as they progress through the elementary grades if the composition of students classified as active ELs in the publicly reported statistics is constantly changing.

The best way to understand the average performance of the EL students, and the work that schools do to support ELs in their acquisition of academic skills, is to look at all students who began their schooling as ELs together. Practitioners and families might find these statistics more useful in understanding what to expect when a student begins as an EL. When we look at the data that way, the performance of students who were never classified as ELs and of students who

at some point have been classified as ELs is very similar (**see the right panel of Figure A**).

This simple example illustrates that each method of reporting the performance of ELs serves a different purpose. We aim to paint a more complete picture of EL performance, and therefore include former ELs in our analyses of ELs' academic performance—either as their own subgroup or as members of our "Began as EL" subgroup (which also includes active ELs).

FIGURE A

Reporting Only Active English Learners Misses How Well Most English Learners Perform

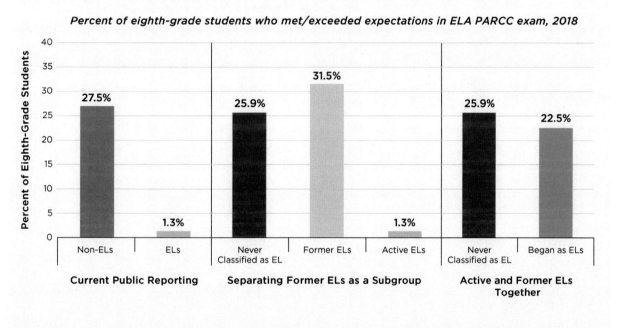

Percent of eighth-grade students who met/exceeded expectations in ELA PARCC exam, 2018

Advocates and scholars have been raising these issues since the introduction of NCLB and have proposed other supplemental ways of reporting the performance of ELs.[9] There are now some states that are considering reporting new subgroups, including former EL students, as a way of understanding the progress of students after they demonstrate proficiency in English according to the test offered. This would allow us a better understanding of the effectiveness of programs that support ELs. But while this would show the performance of ELs that had successfully demonstrated English proficiency on

the test, it still would not accurately show the growth in academic performance of ELs as a whole, since the group of former ELs changes every year and does not include students who have not gained proficiency. Others have called for reporting the total EL group, which includes all students who at some point were classified as ELs. This avoids the bias that is introduced by selecting only students who have or have not successfully gained proficiency, but it still mixes the performance of new ELs arriving to the district with the performance of students who have been ELs for many years.[10]

---

9 Hopkins, Thompson, Linquanti, Hakuta, & August (2013).
10 See box titled "Different Pictures on EL Performance,

Depending on How Students are Grouped" on p.6-7 for an example of different ways of reporting data on ELs.

Thus, there are concerns and questions about how well ELs are performing academically in school, but there is a lack of accurate information to gauge how they are doing relative to students who enter school as native English speakers or already proficient in English. Therefore, this study examines how cohorts of ELs progressed in CPS as they moved from kindergarten through the elementary and middle grades in an less biased way—looking at the same EL students over time relative to students who were never classified as ELs.

Furthermore, there is also little information on how ELs are performing on measures of achievement other than test scores, yet grades and attendance are highly predictive of educational attainment—even more so than test scores.[11] Hence, this study examines multiple outcomes, asking:

- How did the academic performance (in attendance, test scores, grades, and Freshman OnTrack rates) of students who entered kindergarten as ELs compare to students who entered kindergarten as proficient or native English speakers over time?

- How did students who entered kindergarten as ELs progress toward English proficiency?

- What differentiates students who did not demonstrate English proficiency by the end of eighth grade, and how was their academic performance different from other ELs?

This descriptive study draws on data from more than 18,000 students who began as ELs among three cohorts, who were continuously-enrolled in CPS from kindergarten to eighth grade. Chapter 1 introduces how students were identified as ELs in CPS and the services and policies that applied to them. Chapter 2 describes the academic trajectories of all students who began kindergarten as ELs and how they compared to students never classified as ELs in attendance, test scores, and grades, and whether they were on-track to graduate high school in ninth grade. Chapter 3 focuses on understanding the time it took ELs to reach English proficiency. Chapter 4 describes the difference in performance among ELs based on whether or not they demonstrated proficiency, highlighting the experiences of students who remained active ELs as they entered high school. Finally, we conclude with an interpretive summary.

---

11 Gottfried (2010); Allensworth & Easton (2007); Allensworth, Gwynne, Moore, & de la Torre (2014).

CHAPTER 1

English Learners in CPS: Policies & Characteristics

Throughout Chicago's history, the city and its schools have been home to many whose first language was not English. In 1870, Chicago had the largest foreign-born population of any American city,[12] and as early as 1865, German-speaking parents demanded German language instruction for their children in CPS.[13] Over 150 years later, in the 2018-19 school year, one out of every four CPS kindergartners was not fluent in English. If supported in their language development, these students' proficiency in multiple languages could be an asset for Chicago's future. How CPS identifies and supports students who are learning English is crucial to their academic success, and the success of the district as a whole.

In this chapter, we will discuss the educational system that ELs in CPS navigate. This includes the history of EL education in Chicago, the current system for identifying and monitoring ELs, and the academic and linguistic supports mandated by state law. Then, we will look more closely at the three cohorts of ELs in CPS for whom we analyzed data, from their kindergarten year until they completed eighth grade.

History of Bilingual Education in CPS

As a city founded on immigration, Chicago has educated students still learning English throughout the city's history. In the mid-nineteenth century, many parochial schools in ethnically-concentrated neighborhoods offered instruction solely in students' native languages, and public schools, responding to the concerns of German immigrants, offered German language instruction to about one-fourth of all students in the district.[14] In 1898, the mayor-commissioned Harper Report

expressed concerns about public schools "where a large proportion of the school children comes from families to whom English is barely known."[15] At that time, German and Polish would have been the most common non-English languages spoken in Chicago.[16]

Despite its long tradition of serving students who were not native-English speakers, CPS has also struggled throughout its history to adequately support these students. In 1968, Latino students in several Chicago high schools joined Black students in organized school walkouts aimed at creating better school conditions for students of color. Central to the demands of Latino students was that their schools hire "qualified bilingual Latin-American teachers," because their current language needs were being unmet. This student protest was part of a long history of activism from members of Chicago's Latino community seeking "high quality bilingual instruction" for Spanish-speaking students.[17]

In 1980, the desegregation consent decree between CPS and the federal government ordered that the district "promptly implement a plan to ensure that non- and limited- English speaking students are provided with the instructional services necessary to assure their effective participation in the educational programs of the Chicago School District."[18] In 2009, when the consent decree was lifted, Chicago's EL services were still found by the Department of Justice to be inadequate.[19]

In recent years, the Illinois State Board of Education and CPS have sought to build on the strengths of ELs by creating seals of biliteracy. The State Seal of Biliteracy, introduced in 2014, recognizes Illinois high school graduates who have gained proficiency in one or more

---

12 Paral (2003).
13 Herrick (1971).
14 Herrick (1971).
15 Herrick (1971).
16 Buck (1903).
17 Alanís (2010).

18 United States of America v. Board of Education of the City of Chicago (1980).
19 The consent decree was lifted despite the deficiencies in the district's EL services because the decree's bilingual education requirements duplicated provisions already present in Illinois state law. United States of America v. Board of Education of the City of Chicago (2009).

languages in addition to English by their senior year of high school.[20] In 2018, 1,720 CPS graduates earned the State Seal of Biliteracy.[21] The district also offers the CPS Seal of Biliteracy, which recognizes elementary and middle school students who are working toward biliteracy in preparation for high school.[22]

English Learners in Chicago Today

Who Is an English Learner?

Active English Learners are students who have a non-English language background, and whose English proficiency is not sufficient for them to "participate fully in the school setting." [23] Once an English Learner demonstrates proficiency, they are considered a former English Learner.

How Does CPS Identify English Learners?

When a student enters CPS, if their parent or guardian indicates that the student speaks a language other than English, the student is screened for English proficiency within 30 days of enrollment. If the student scores above the state-determined cut point on the screener, they are considered English proficient. If the student does not pass the screener, they are considered an English Learner.

What Supports Do English Learners Receive?

In Illinois, schools' legal obligations regarding the instruction and language development of ELs depend on how many students speaking the same language attend their school. If 20 or more students with the same language background attend, the school is required to offer a program following the Transitional Bilingual Education (TBE) model. This model includes instruction in both English and the students' native language. If fewer than 20 students with the same language background attend, students are to receive a program following the Transitional Program of Instruction (TPI) model. Under this model, ELs receive English language development, but might not receive instruction in their native language.[24]

A popular option for the instruction of ELs which satisfies state requirements is the Dual Language Education (DLE) model. In programs using this model, all students, including both English-proficient students and ELs, receive core instruction in both English and the target language, usually Spanish. Students also receive language development in the language they do not speak.[25]

While these are the models of bilingual education that meet the state's legal requirements for ELs, past audits suggest that many CPS schools may not be in compliance with state law in terms of their services for ELs.[26] That is, ELs might not receive the academic and linguistic supports that state law requires to support their development.

Previous research suggests that the type of services that ELs receive (i.e., dual immersion, English only, etc.) significantly impacts their linguistic and academic growth.[27] Describing the type of services CPS students receive falls beyond the scope of this report, but future Consortium work will seek to examine how these services impact student outcomes.

How Do English Learners Demonstrate English Proficiency?

To determine if they have gained English proficiency, each year ELs complete the "ACCESS for ELLs" test. This exam tests a student's proficiency in English reading, writing, speaking, and listening; it is typically administered in late January or early February. The exam takes into account the student's grade in school, meaning that, for example, a third-grader is expected to show stronger English skills than a second-grader in order to demonstrate proficiency. When a student scores above the state-determined cut score on the ACCESS, they are considered English proficient, which means they are no longer an active EL.

In Illinois, ACCESS cut scores have changed three times in the last decade, as shown in **Figure 1**. This means that in some years, it may have been more difficult for students to demonstrate proficiency than

---

20 Illinois State Board of Education (2018b).
21 Chicago Public Schools (2018, June 4).
22 Chicago Public Schools (n.d.), Seal of biliteracy.
23 Illinois Admin. Code tit. 23, § 228.10 (2017).

24 Chicago Public Schools SY 17-18 Bilingual Education Handbook.
25 Chicago Public Schools (n.d.), Language and cultural education.
26 Belsha (2017, June 28).
27 Valentino & Reardon (2015).

FIGURE 1

ACCESS Test and Cut Score Changes

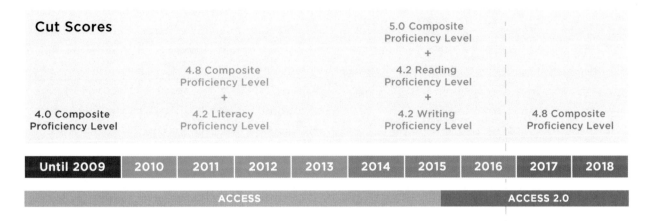

in others. Additionally, the ACCESS test itself was changed in the 2015-16 school year to better align to the language proficiency necessary for college and career readiness, and the test's standards changed in the 2016-17 school year, which required students to demonstrate more skills to be considered proficient, resulting in fewer students being classified as proficient.

ELs in grades 1-12 who have significant cognitive disabilities can take the alternate ACCESS, a modified version of the exam. However, in the 2016-17 school year, only 2 percent of CPS ELs who were also identified as having a disability took the alternate ACCESS, while 96 percent of such students took the standard ACCESS test.[28] Students taking the alternate ACCESS have no opportunity to demonstrate English proficiency because the exam's proficiency levels are lower than the state-determined proficiency cut-score.[29] ELs with disabilities taking the regular ACCESS must reach the same state-determined cut score as other ELs in order to demonstrate proficiency.

Not All English Learners Receive Services

Not all CPS students who are developing in English proficiency receive services to aid their language development. Parents and guardians may refuse services for their child, which would prevent students from participating in the EL services their school offers. Even though these students do not receive services, they are still considered ELs, and continue to take the ACCESS test of English proficiency each year.

Audits of CPS schools have also shown that many schools have not always been in compliance with state legal requirements, which means that students at these schools who are enrolled in bilingual education services might not actually be receiving mandated services. In 2016, for example, 71 percent of schools audited did not provide the level of EL services mandated by state law.[30] This doesn't necessarily mean that students at these schools do not receive any EL services, but it remains troubling that many CPS schools have not been

---

28 Two percent of English Learners with disabilities were not tested on either form of the ACCESS in 2017. This rate matches the percent of English Learners without identified disabilities who were not ACCESS-tested in 2017.

29 The proficiency level range of the Alternate ACCESS does not exceed 3.0 for any language domain. Therefore, any student assessed with this test will not be able to meet the

state's English proficiency criteria, which currently requires students to score above a 4.8 composite proficiency level to be considered English proficient. For more information see https://www.isbe.net/Documents/Alternate_ACCESS_Guid-ance_and_Documentation_2017-18.pdf

30 Belsha (2017, June 28).

supporting ELs, a group from whom much is expected, to the degree legally required. The audits of EL services suggested that charter schools in CPS were more likely than traditional schools to be out of compliance with state mandates on EL services.[31] The large number of CPS schools out of compliance with state mandates may suggest that schools require additional resources to adequately meet the needs of ELs.

CPS Policies Affecting English Learners

CPS policies related to grading and retention are modified for ELs to accommodate for students' lack of English proficiency. For example, in 2016, the CPS Board of Education introduced a grading protocol for ELs which mandated that "No English Learner shall receive a failing grade due to limited English proficiency."[32] That is, if an EL is taking a class taught in English, the student's lack of proficiency cannot be allowed to cause the student to fail.

Additionally, elementary grade promotion policies differ for active ELs. In CPS, elementary grade retention and promotion decisions are typically made on the basis of standardized test results, grades, and attendance. For active ELs, decisions about grade retention and promotion are made entirely based on grades and attendance, with standardized testing results ineligible for consideration.[33] As the standardized tests administered in CPS are almost always in English, this policy serves to accommodate for the student's lack of English proficiency. In high school, grade promotion requirements are identical for both ELs and non-ELs.[34]

English Learners in This Study

This study focuses on the academic performance of consistent cohorts of students over time, starting with students who began as ELs in kindergarten, and compares them to students who began kindergarten in the same years, but were not classified as ELs. Instead of focusing on active ELs, a group that changes each year, studying this consistent group of students who began as ELs allows us to see their growth over time, even if they demonstrated proficiency and became former ELs. This will allow us to better understand the school experiences of the typical EL, the average CPS student who was classified as an EL in their kindergarten year. We consider the aggregated outcomes of all students who began as ELs to represent the experiences and performance of the typical English Learner.

Our sample includes three cohorts of students who were first-time kindergartners in 2007-08, 2008-09, and 2009-10 and remained enrolled in CPS each year through the school year in which they would be expected to reach the eighth grade (2015-16, 2016-17, and 2017-18, respectively).[35] If students were retained in a grade, or skipped a grade, they remained in the sample with their original kindergarten cohort.

We keep only continuously-enrolled students so that we can follow the same group of students over time. While this strategy allows us to understand student growth without bias from students exiting and entering as ELs, it does exclude students who moved in and out of CPS, and students who entered CPS in later grades. For ELs, this excluded group would include recent immigrants who may have had different linguistic needs than ELs who began CPS in kindergarten. Our results would not apply to such students, and we hope to study their academic performance in a later study.

About two-thirds (66.4 percent) of first-time kindergartners in 2008, 2009, and 2010 remained enrolled in CPS every year through the expected eighth-grade year. Kindergartners who began as ELs were more likely to remain enrolled in CPS than students who were never classified as ELs (76 percent vs. 63 percent).[36]

---

31 Belsha (2017, June 28).

32 Chicago Public Schools Policy Manual, Section 603.1. 2016.

33 Chicago Public Schools Policy Manual, Section 605.2. 2009.

34 Chicago Public Schools Policy Manual, Section 605.1. 2018.

35 See Appendix A for a description of the data used in the study and a description of the sample.

36 Students who were never classified as ELs were more likely to be affected by the school closings of 2013, in which CPS closed 47 elementary schools serving primarily Black students. The students in our sample would have been finishing third through fifth grade at this time. The experience of school closings may have influenced families' decisions to leave CPS, and could explain some of the difference in consistent enrollment between students who began as ELs and students never classified as ELs. However, when we only look at students who did not attend a school that closed in 2013, or only look at Latino students, who were less likely to be affected by the school closings, we still find that students who began as ELs were still significantly more likely to be continuously-enrolled in CPS from K-8, compared to students never classified as ELs.

We identify students in our sample as ELs based on whether they took the ACCESS test of English proficiency,[37] and whether they reached proficiency on the test—not whether they were actually receiving services. Because ACCESS is required by the state for all ELs, this allows us to follow both ELs who received services and those who did not. Describing the services students received falls beyond the scope of this study, but in future work the UChicago Consortium plans to examine the role of EL services on academic growth.

Sample Demographics

Our sample of three kindergarten cohorts includes 53,125 students, including students who began as ELs and students who were never classified as ELs (**see Table 1**). About one-third of continuously-enrolled CPS students in these cohorts began as ELs.[38]

Students who entered kindergarten as ELs were much more likely to be Latino, whereas students who were never classified as ELs were much more likely to be Black. ELs were also much more likely to be eligible for free or reduced-price lunch. They were about as likely as students who were never classified as ELs to attend CPS preschools.

Switching schools can negatively impact student outcomes like test scores and high school graduation.[39] Among continuously-enrolled students, ELs were less likely to switch schools: 13 percent of students who

TABLE 1

Sample Demographics by EL Status

	Began as English Learners	Never Classified as English Learners	Overall Sample
Number	18,264	34,861	53,125
Male	51%	50%	50%
Latino	90%	33%	52%
Black	1%	52%	35%
Eligible for Free/ Reduced-Price Lunch	94%	82%	86%
Attended CPS Pre-K	64%	66%	65%
Attended More than 2 Schools from K-8	13%	24%	20%
Had an IEP:			
...in Kindergarten	7%	5%	6%
...in Third Grade	11%	10%	10%
...in Eighth Grade	17%	15%	16%
Attended Charter School:			
...in Kindergarten	4%	7%	6%
...in Third Grade	7%	9%	8%
...in Eighth Grade	12%	13%	13%

Note: Overall sample is comprised of three cohorts of students who were first-time kindergartners in 2007-08, 2008-09, and 2009-10 and remained enrolled in CPS each year through the school year in which they would be expected to reach the eighth grade (2015-16, 2016-17, and 2017-18, respectively).

37 For our "Began as English Learner" category, we include all continuously-enrolled CPS students who were classified as ELs during their elementary years, as defined by taking the ACCESS test of English proficiency. Ninety-five percent of these students took the ACCESS test in kindergarten, 99 percent took the test by the first grade, and 99.6 percent took the test by the end of second grade. Active ELs might not take the ACCESS in a given year because they were absent during test administration or because their school had issues in administering the test. In fact, we find that an EL's attendance predicts whether the student took the test in a given year. We also find that ELs who were identified as having special needs were less

likely to take the ACCESS in a given year.

38 Thirty-four percent of our sample of 53,125 students who began kindergarten in CPS in 2008, 2009, or 2010 began as ELs. Because kindergartners who began as ELs were more likely to be continuously-enrolled and thus remain in our sample, this proportion of ELs is higher in our sample than in the general population of CPS kindergartners, where, in the 2017-18 school year, 27 percent of kindergartners were active ELs. Additionally, some ELs also enter CPS later than kindergarten, and 33 percent of all K-12 CPS students in the 2017-18 school year were former or active ELs.

39 Rumberger (2015).

began as ELs attended more than two schools during their K-8 years, compared to 24 percent of students who were never classified as ELs. Students never classified as ELs were more likely to attend schools that CPS closed, which seems to contribute to their higher mobility, as they were forced to switch schools.[40]

Researchers and advocates have raised concerns that ELs may be overidentified for special education services compared to the general population of students.[41] Our results do not support this theory: over the course of their academic careers, continuously-enrolled CPS students who began as ELs were identified as needing IEPs at similar rates to students who were never classified as ELs. However, we do find that students who began as ELs and were eventually identified as having special needs demonstrated proficiency at much lower rates; see Chapter 4 for more details. Students with IEPs who began as ELs were more likely to be identified as having a learning disability compared to students with an IEP who were never classified as ELs (75 percent vs. 65 percent of students with IEPs), and less likely to be identified as having an emotional and behavioral disorder (3 percent vs. 7 percent of students with IEPs).

As previously noted, there is some evidence that charter schools may have been less likely to provide mandated bilingual education services during the time when the students in our sample started attending CPS.[42] Our results show that continuously-enrolled ELs were actually slightly less likely to attend charter schools in kindergarten and third grade, although they attended charter schools at the same rates as other students by their eighth grade year.

TABLE 2

Linguistic Composition of Sample

Language	N	Percentage	Median Kindergarten Composite Proficiency Level	Percentage Eligible for Free/ Reduced-Price Lunch	Attended CPS Pre-K	Number of Schools Represented in Kindergarten	Median # of Same-Language Kindergarten Classmates Within the Same School
Spanish	16,396	89.8%	1.6	96%	64%	295	72
Polish	343	1.9%	1.9	57%	43%	53	10
Cantonese	263	1.4%	2.1	93%	85%	38	20
Arabic	154	0.8%	1.9	92%	64%	47	4
Vietnamese	145	0.8%	1.9	79%	73%	40	4
Urdu	142	0.8%	2.9	88%	70%	29	10
Tagalog	101	0.6%	2.6	68%	62%	49	1
Other Language (n<50)	720	3.9%	1.9	76%	62%	167	2
Began as ELs	18,264	100%	1.7	94%	64%	311	65

Note: The last column represents the number of same-language kindergarten classmates the median student of that linguistic background had in their school. For example, the median Arabic-speaking kindergartner in our sample had four kindergarten classmates at their school who also spoke Arabic.

40 Students who were never classified as English Learners were more likely to be affected by the school closings of 2013, in which CPS closed 47 elementary schools primarily serving Black students in the same year. The students in our sample would have been finishing third through fifth grade at this time. This means that some of the difference in the number of CPS schools students attended during their K-8 years was due to students being forced to attend a different school. While the closings undoubtedly influenced the number of schools students attended, when we only look at students who did not attend a school that closed in 2013, or only look at Latino students, who were less likely to be affected by the school closings, we still find that students who began as ELs were less likely to attend more than two schools in CPS from K-8 compared to students never classified as ELs.

41 Colorín Colorado (n.d.); Mid-Atlantic Equity Consortium (2016).

42 Belsha (2017, June 28).

Linguistic Composition of Sample

Of the 18,000 continuously-enrolled ELs in our sample, the overwhelming majority (90 percent) were Spanish speakers (**see Table 2**).[43] Polish and Cantonese were the next most common languages—no other language made up more than 1 percent of continuously-enrolled ELs. In total, 77 different languages were represented in our sample. Of the different linguistic groups, Spanish speakers were the most likely to be eligible for free or reduced-price lunch and also began with the lowest initial level of English proficiency, as measured by their scores on the kindergarten ACCESS test.

Summary

CPS has a long history of serving bilingual students, but has not always provided the services the state requires to support these students in their academic and linguistic development. Our study follows more than 18,000 students who began as ELs in three cohorts of students who completed eighth grade in 2017-18. While the vast majority of these students were Spanish speakers, more than 70 languages were represented. Importantly, more than one-third of continuously-enrolled CPS students began as ELs. Thus, it is critical to understand their trajectory for the academic benefit of these students, and to understand what is needed in classrooms, schools, and the district as a whole to continue supporting them.

---

43 Spanish speakers were more likely to remain in CPS and thus be in our sample. Students who spoke Polish, Arabic, and Urdu were more likely to leave CPS at some point after kindergarten, which would remove them from the sample, as we are looking strictly at students with continuous records. However, the percentage of Spanish speakers in our sample matches closely to the general sample of kindergarten ELs, including students who were not continuously-enrolled (87 percent vs. 90 percent of continuously-enrolled ELs).

CHAPTER 2

Beginning as English Learners: Academic Performance

National and state reports on the academic performance of ELs show that this group of students is lagging behind in reading and math achievement when compared to non-ELs.[44] However, as previously mentioned, these reports only focus on students who are active ELs in a given year, providing a partial view of the performance of students who begin as ELs. Reporting on the outcomes of only active ELs misses how well most ELs perform since former ELs (those who were ELs at some point but successfully demonstrated English proficiency) are not counted as part of the EL group on these metrics.

By contrast, the approach adopted in this study allows us to examine the academic trajectories of ELs by considering all students who entered school as ELs in kindergarten and following the same group of students through their elementary careers. As shown earlier (see Figure A in the Introduction, on p.7), separating active and former ELs into different reporting groups provides a very different picture than the two groups combined. We look at the outcomes of all students who began as ELs together, regardless of when and whether they achieved English proficiency, to gain understanding about the school outcomes of the typical EL, the average student who began as an EL in CPS. At the district level, this helps us understand how ELs in CPS are doing in school, but if this approach were applied at the school level, it would give parents and school leaders a better sense of how successful their school is at educating and supporting ELs. In Chapter 4, we then separate students who began as ELs based on whether they demonstrated English proficiency on the ACCESS test by the end of eighth grade.

To preview the findings in this chapter, we found that students who began as ELs had higher attendance rates, similar rates of improvement on standardized tests, comparable grades in core subjects, and equal prospects of being on-track to graduate from high

school once they reached ninth grade, compared to students never classified as ELs. This is a very different perspective on the performance of ELs than the one provided by statistics that exclude students once they reach English proficiency.

Attendance

Students who began as ELs had higher average attendance rates than their peers who were never classified as ELs across the elementary grades

Figure 2 displays attendance rates from kindergarten to eighth grade for students who began as ELs and students who were never classified as ELs. On average, throughout elementary school, students who began as ELs were more likely to regularly attend school than students who were never classified as ELs. For instance, in third grade, the average student in the EL group was present 97 percent of days, which means they missed three fewer days of school, on average, than their peers never classified as EL.

FIGURE 2

Attendance Gap Narrowed over Time, but Attendance Rates Remained Higher for Students who Began as ELs

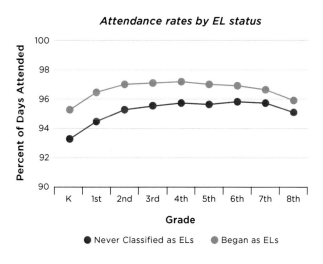

Attendance rates by EL status

● Never Classified as ELs　　● Began as ELs

---

44 U.S. Department of Education (n.d); Illinois Report Card 2017-2018 (n.d.).

Over time, the attendance gap narrowed as students move into higher grades, but attendance remained higher for students who began as ELs. By the time students who began as ELs reached eighth grade, they were attending 96 percent of school days (missing seven days/year, on average), whereas students who were never classified as ELs were attending 95 percent of school days (missing nine days/year, on average). These attendance rates for both groups are lower than we would hope.[45] However, students who began as ELs were attending, on average, two more days of school than the average CPS eighth-grader.[46]

Research has shown that students need to attend school regularly in order to succeed. Absenteeism, particularly chronic absenteeism (missing 10 percent or more school days, as defined in Illinois), can have detrimental consequences on student academic performance. For instance, early absenteeism has been found to be negatively related to academic and behavioral kindergarten readiness,[47] as well as achievement in math and reading in early elementary grades.[48] Additionally, students with poor attendance in the middle grades are more likely to fail courses and be off-track to graduate from high school.[49]

Furthermore, absenteeism has been recognized as a relevant issue nationwide. In many states, including Illinois, student attendance has been adopted as an accountability measure of student progress. Considering the importance of attendance for student learning, in CPS, it is encouraging to find that continuously-enrolled students who begin as ELs have relatively strong attendance.

Standardized Test Scores

CPS requires that, districtwide, all students in second to eighth grade take the NWEA-MAP in math and reading during the spring semester.[50] Because NWEA-MAP was first implemented in Chicago in 2013, students from the 2008 and 2009 cohorts were only tested in grades 5-8 and 4-8, respectively. **Figures 3 and 4** show NWEA-MAP math and reading test scores and gains for the 2010 kindergarten cohort, who took the test from third through eighth grade. The 2008 and 2009 cohorts show similar trends for the grade levels in which they took the NWEA-MAP and can be found in **Appendix B**.

Students who began as ELs grew similarly on math standardized tests compared to their peers who were never classified as ELs

In math, students who began as ELs scored slightly below students who were never classified as ELs (**see Figure 3A**). For example, in third grade, the average student who was never classified as EL was scoring at the 45th percentile, while the average EL student was scoring at the 40th percentile. However, over time, students who began as ELs had similar math growth trajectories as their peers who were never classified as ELs.

Figure 3B also shows the average gain score of the two groups of students. Gain scores represent the point difference in NWEA-MAP scores from one year to the next. For example, if a student scored 200 points on the NWEA-MAP in third grade and 210 points on the NWEA-MAP in fourth grade, their gain score would be 10. On average, students who began as ELs improved at a similar rate to their peers never classified as ELs in the NWEA-MAP

---

45 Balfanz and Byrnes (2012) define regular attendance as students missing five or fewer days of school in a given year.

46 According to the metrics reported by CPS, the average daily attendance rate for eight-grade students has been 95 percent for 2016, 2017, and 2018 school years. See https://cps.edu/SchoolData/Pages/SchoolData.aspx

47 Ehrlich, Gwynne, & Allensworth (2018).

48 Romero & Lee (2007); Chang & Romero (2008).

49 Allensworth et al. (2014).

50 CPS also requires that all ELs with a literacy composite score of 3.0 or higher on the ACCESS test take the NWEA-MAP assessment in the spring. In our sample, students who began as ELs took the NWEA-MAP at similar rates than students

who were never ELs. For example, in the fifth grade, 96 percent of students who began as ELs took the NWEA-MAP reading exam, compared to 95 percent of students who were never classified as ELs. Although ELs with lower levels of English proficiency (i.e., ACCESS literacy proficiency levels of less than 3.5) were less likely to take the NWEA-MAP, still 85 percent of such students took the test in fifth grade. Also, although the NWEA-MAP assessment has a Spanish version, in CPS few schools administer the Spanish version and it is only available for the math section. For example, from our sample only 0.35 percent of students who began as ELs ever took the Spanish version of the math NWEA-MAP.

spring assessment from year to year. For example, from third to fourth grade, students who began as ELs had a 10-point scale score gain compared to students who were never classified as ELs who had an 11-point scale score gain. In the middle grades, both groups had an average math score gain of approximately 6 scale score points.

Students who began as ELs grew at a faster rate in reading than their peers never classified as ELs

Figure 4 displays test scores and gains on the NWEA-MAP reading assessment from third to eighth grade among students in the 2010 cohort who began as ELs and those who were never classified as ELs.

Differences in reading performance on the exam—which was given in English—was wider than in math. Students who began as ELs initially had lower reading scores than their peers who were never classified as ELs, but by the end of elementary school, the difference was narrower (**see Figure 4a**). The difference in the percentile rank between students who began as ELs and those who were never classified as ELs narrowed from 14 percentile points in third grade to 8 percentile points by the time students reached eighth grade. As students in the EL group progress across grades, their English skills are expected to improve, which may explain the reading score growth we observe. At the

FIGURE 3

Students Who Began as ELs had Similar Growth Trajectories and Gains on Math NWEA-MAP Test Compared to Students Never Classified as ELs

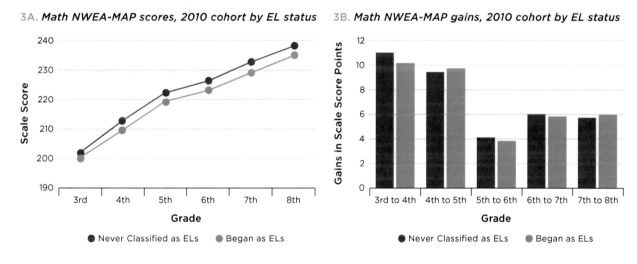

3A. *Math NWEA-MAP scores, 2010 cohort by EL status*

3B. *Math NWEA-MAP gains, 2010 cohort by EL status*

FIGURE 4

Students Who Began as ELs Grew at a Slightly Faster Rate and had Slightly Larger Gains on the Reading NWEA-MAP Test than Students Never Classified as ELs

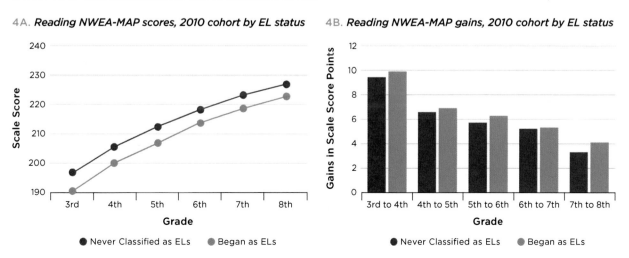

4A. *Reading NWEA-MAP scores, 2010 cohort by EL status*

4B. *Reading NWEA-MAP gains, 2010 cohort by EL status*

beginning of third grade, around 80 percent of students who began as ELs were still active ELs.[51]

Over time, students who began as ELs had slightly larger gains in reading test scores than students who were never classified as ELs (**see Figure 4b**). For example, from third to fourth grade, students who began as ELs were gaining 1 scale score point more than their peers who were never classified as ELs, on average.

English Learners' Performance in a Context of District Improvement

CPS has received considerable attention over the last several years for students' academic progress. A nationally-representative study on students' standardized test scores between 2009 and 2014 found that CPS students were learning and growing faster than 96 percent of U.S. school districts. These results held true for students across different cohorts and racial/ethnic and socioeconomic sub-groups.[D] Similarly, we find that ELs in CPS are demonstrating strong performance and growth when compared to national trends, as are students who are never classified as ELs. This box highlights ELs' outstanding academic achievement on NWEA-MAP, not only when compared to other students in the district but also relative to the average student in the country.

Figure B displays the percentage of students from the 2010 kindergarten cohort who scored at or above the nationwide 50th percentile on the NWEA-MAP assessments. If students in CPS were scoring very similarly to students across the country, we would expect that 50 percent of CPS students were scoring at or above the 50th percentile. In third grade, students in our sample were scoring below average on the NWEA-MAP: fewer than one-half of students who began as ELs and students who were never classified as ELs scored at or above the 50th percentile nationally on the test in either math or reading. However, over the course of five years, students in our sample were growing more than other students across the nation, such that by the end of elementary school, over one-half of the eighth-graders in both groups scored above the national average in both math and reading.

Students are expected to grow in their skills and knowledge from year to year, but moving ahead of other students their age is uncommon. The fact that Chicago students are pulling ahead of other students across the nation is remarkable, and this progress occurred for both students who began as ELs and those who were never classified as ELs. CPS students who began as ELs grew significantly in their reading scores, compared to the national average. In the third grade, only 27 percent of CPS students who began as ELs scored above the 50th percentile, while in the eighth grade, 60 percent scored above the 50th percentile.

FIGURE B

ELs Demonstrated Strong Performance and Growth, with Respect to the National Average

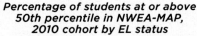

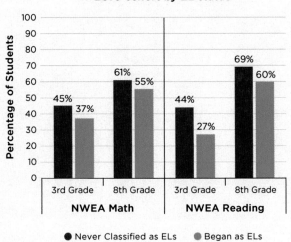

Percentage of students at or above 50th percentile in NWEA-MAP, 2010 cohort by EL status

---

D   Reardon & Hinze-Pifer (2017).

---

51 See next chapter for a detailed description of ELs' trajectories toward English proficiency.

Course Grades (GPA)

Students who began as ELs had similar GPAs to students never classified as ELs

Figure 5 shows GPA in core subjects (math, English, science, and social studies) from second to eighth grade, among students attending non-charter schools.[52] Students who began as ELs received very similar grades to students who were never classified as ELs in core subjects. For instance, in second grade, students who began as ELs received, on average, a slightly lower GPA than students who were never classified as ELs (2.87 vs. 2.95, respectively). However, in eighth grade, those who began as ELs attained a slightly higher GPA, on average (2.93 vs. 2.91 for students never classified as ELs). Over time, students in both groups were earning just under a B- average in core course grades.

Previous research has shown that middle grades GPA is the strongest predictor for Freshman OnTrack status[53] and high school performance.[54] Thus, it is encouraging to find that ELs were performing similarly to their peers never classified as ELs in core subjects, even though their reading test scores were lower than those of never classified ELs. Higher attendance rates among EL students likely helped to bolster their performance in their classes.

We also examined students' GPA in math and reading separately since grades in these two subjects were counted toward the academic performance requirement for EL promotion decisions.[55]

Students who began as ELs had similar GPAs in math to students never classified as ELs

Math GPAs among students attending non-charter schools between second and eighth grade are shown in Figure 6. Grades in math were a bit lower than core GPAs, and math grades slightly decreased between second and eighth grade for students in both groups. However, this decline in math grades is larger for students who were never classified as ELs (0.15 points vs. 0.05). Both groups of students started out in second grade with almost the same math GPA (2.73 for began as ELs and 2.74 for never classified as ELs) but by the eighth grade, those who began as ELs had, on average, a slightly stronger math GPA (2.68 for began as ELs and 2.59 for never classified as ELs).

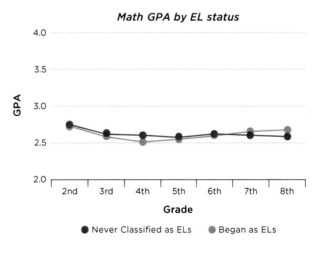

FIGURE 5

Students Who Began as ELs Received Similar Grades to Students Never Classified as ELs in Core Subjects

GPA in core classes by EL status

● Never Classified as ELs   ● Began as ELs

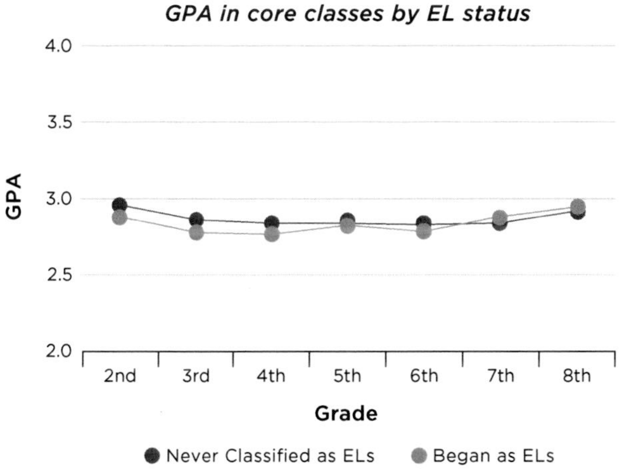

Note: Core classes include math, English, science and social studies.

FIGURE 6

Elementary Students Who Began as ELs Received Similar Grades in Math to Students Never Classified as ELs

Math GPA by EL status

● Never Classified as ELs   ● Began as ELs

---

52 Many CPS charter schools use different student information systems from the IMPACT system used by non-charter schools. Because each system varies in the way that it stores information about courses, credits, teachers, periods, grades, and other data, creating linkages across systems is difficult, and our data archive currently does not include records of charter school students' course performance.

53 The Freshman OnTrack indicator is a metric used in CPS to predict whether a ninth-grader will graduate from high school on time, and is based on course failures and credits. For more information on Freshman OnTrack, see Allensworth & Easton (2005, 2007).
54 Allensworth et al. (2014).
55 Chicago Public Schools Policy Manual, Section 605.2. 2009.

Students who began as ELs had lower reading GPAs in the early grades, but caught up to their peers who were never classified as ELs over time

Figure 7 displays reading GPAs among students attending non-charter schools between second and eighth grade. Similar to what was found for reading standardized test scores, students who began as ELs had comparatively lower average GPAs in reading than their peers who were never classified as ELs when they started elementary school. In second grade, students who began as ELs had an average reading GPA of 2.53, compared to an average reading GPA of 2.66 for students never classified as ELs. However, EL students improved their reading grades over time, eventually catching up to their peers between seventh and eighth grade. For example, in eighth grade, the average reading GPA was 2.79 for students who began as ELs and 2.78 for those who were never classified as ELs.

As previously mentioned, English skills are expected to increase as students progress throughout the grades, and this could underlie the improvements in reading grades over time. Most students demonstrated English proficiency between second and fifth grade on the ACCESS test, a pattern shown later in this report. Similarly, the improvements in reading grades could have been related to CPS's grading policy for ELs that came into effect in 2016. The policy stated that "No English Learner shall receive a failing grade due to limited English proficiency."[56] Hence, some active ELs might have received higher grades or fewer Fs as a way to compensate for their lack of English proficiency.

High School Outcomes

While this study mainly focused on students' academic trajectories from kindergarten to eighth grade, we also examined students' early high school outcomes. For this analysis, we focused on students from the 2008 and 2009 cohorts and examined their status by the time they were expected to be in ninth grade (school years 2016-17 and 2017-18, respectively): whether they were retained in elementary school, left the district or remained in CPS and whether they were on-track to graduate from high school (Freshman OnTrack status).[57]

FIGURE 7

ELs had Lower Reading Grades than Students Never Classified as ELs from Second to Sixth Grade but Caught Up by Middle School

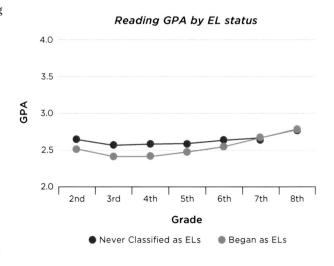

Reading GPA by EL status

● Never Classified as ELs   ● Began as ELs

The Freshman OnTrack indicator identifies students as on-track to graduate if they earn at least five full-year course credits and no more than one semester F in a core course during their first year of high school.[58]

Students who began as ELs were more likely than other students to be enrolled in a CPS high school by the expected ninth-grade year

In the expected ninth-grade year, students who began kindergarten as ELs were less likely to have left CPS for another district, or to have been retained in elementary school than other students. **Figure 8** shows whether students were retained in elementary school, promoted to high school, or left CPS by the expected ninth-grade year. By the time continuously-enrolled students were expected to be freshmen, those who were never classified as ELs were more likely to leave CPS. Only 6 percent of students who began as ELs left CPS for the expected ninth-grade year, compared to 12 percent of students who were never classified as ELs. Additionally, students who were never classified as ELs were more likely to be retained in elementary school: in the year they were expected to be in ninth grade, only 7 percent of students who began as ELs were retained, compared to 13 percent of students never classified as ELs.

---

56 Chicago Public Schools Policy Manual, Section 603.1. 2016.
57 We did not analyze Freshman OnTrack status for students in the 2010 cohort, as these students are expected to be in ninth grade in the 2018-19 school year, for which we did not have data at the time of publication.
58 Allensworth & Easton (2005, 2007).

FIGURE 8

Students Who Began as ELs were Less Likely to be Retained or Leave CPS than Students Never Classified as ELs

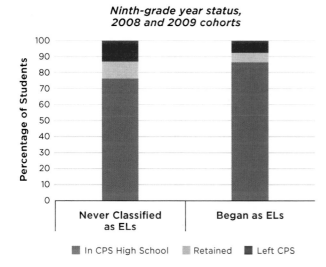

Ninth-grade year status, 2008 and 2009 cohorts

Note: Data from the year in which students were expected to be in ninth grade.

FIGURE 9

In Ninth Grade, Students who Began as ELs were Equally Likely to be On-Track to Graduate from High School as Students Never Classified as ELs

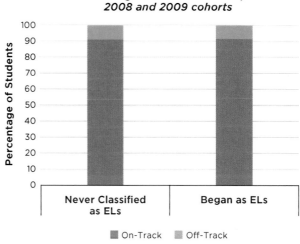

Ninth-grade on-track status, 2008 and 2009 cohorts

Note: Conditional on students being in ninth grade, during the year in which they were expected to be in ninth grade.

As noted in the previous chapter, elementary promotion policies differ for ELs. For these students, test scores in the districtwide assessment (NWEA-MAP) are not considered for grade retention and promotion purposes. Thus, decisions about promoting eighth-graders who were active ELs to high school were based only on their academic performance in math and reading subjects and their attendance.

Among ninth-graders, students who began as ELs were on-track to graduate from high school at the same rate as their peers who were never classified as ELs

Figure 9 displays students' Freshman OnTrack status, conditional on being in ninth grade by the expected year. Students who began as ELs were on-track to graduate from high school at the same rate as students who were never classified as ELs (91 percent). Only nine percent of the students in either group were considered off-track to graduate. Previous Consortium research has shown that being on-track in ninth grade is a stronger predictor of future high school graduation than students' background characteristics and test scores combined.[59] Additionally, previous Consortium research has found that being on-track in ninth grade is as likely to predict high school graduation for active and former ELs as it is for students who are never classified as ELs.[60]

Summary

Looking at all students who began kindergarten as ELs provides a more positive picture of the academic performance and trajectories of the typical EL than what is usually reported. Students who began as ELs had higher attendance rates and earned similar grades compared to students who were never classified as ELs, particularly during the middle grade years. Students who began as ELs also had similar growth trajectories to their peers who were never classified as ELs, both in math and reading on the NWEA-MAP assessments, and, on average, their test scores improved more than those of the average student nationally. Moreover, students who began kindergarten as ELs were less likely to be retained in middle school or leave the district when transitioning to high school and were equally likely as students never classified as ELs to be on-track to graduate on time from high school.

---

59 Allensworth & Easton (2005).
60 Gwynne, Stitziel, Ehrlich & Allensworth (2012).

CHAPTER 3

How Did English Learners Move Toward Proficiency?

In the previous chapter, we examined all students who began CPS as ELs together. This strategy provides an unbiased understanding of how the typical student who enters CPS as an EL performs in school. However, students who begin as ELs make up a large and diverse group, with different trajectories toward English proficiency, and focusing on the typical EL can obscure the experiences of EL students who struggle the most to demonstrate English proficiency. This chapter examines EL students' progression toward English proficiency, as well as the characteristics of EL students who did not reach proficiency on the ACCESS exam before high school. Chapter 4 will draw further attention to students who struggled to perform well on the ACCESS test by examining the academic performance of ELs based on whether they demonstrated English proficiency by the end of eighth grade.

While younger individuals are typically quicker to learn new languages,[61] gaining academic proficiency in a non-native language takes time for most students. Previous studies have indicated that, typically, students take between 3-7 years to develop the academic English skills necessary to demonstrate proficiency.[62]

Importantly, proficiency is not based on whether the student speaks or understands English in their day-to-day life, but is determined by whether the student is able to pass a yearly test demonstrating academic English skills. Research has shown that the academic English necessary to demonstrate proficiency on a test tends to develop later than proficiency in English speaking. For example, a study of two school districts in California found that academic English proficiency took 4-7 years to develop, while oral English proficiency developed within 3-5 years.[63] Many factors, including family income and disability status, influence how long an EL spends working toward proficiency.[64]

In Illinois, an EL demonstrates English proficiency by scoring above the state-determined cut point on the ACCESS test, which tests students on reading, writing, listening, and speaking. The two factors that define proficiency—the ACCESS test and the state-determined cut score—have changed multiple times in the last decade (see Chapter 1), meaning that in some years, it may have been more difficult for ELs to demonstrate proficiency than in other years.

Proportion of Students Who Reached Proficiency: Kindergarten through Eighth Grade

Most of the continuously-enrolled students who began as ELs in kindergarten in our sample eventually demonstrated English proficiency and became former ELs. On their kindergarten ACCESS test, 3 percent of the students who began as ELs demonstrated proficiency (see Figure 10). This means that in their first-grade year, these students would not be considered ELs. The number of former ELs increased over time. By the end of second grade, one in five students who began as ELs in kindergarten demonstrated proficiency and became former ELs. Third grade is when the largest group of students who began as ELs demonstrated proficiency, and more than one-half of students who began as ELs demonstrated proficiency by the end of third grade. Additional students demonstrated proficiency in fourth and fifth grade, such that more than three-fourths of students who began as ELs demonstrated proficiency and became former ELs by the end of fifth grade.

Students who were not proficient by the end of fifth grade were unlikely to demonstrate proficiency during middle school. Of the 4,274 students in the sample who did not demonstrate proficiency by the end of fifth grade,

---

61 Conger (2009); Johnson & Newport (1989).
62 Greenberg Motamedi, Singh, & Thompson (2016); Hakuta, Butler, & Witt (2000); Lin & Neild (2017).
63 Hakuta et al. (2000).
64 Halle, Hair, Wandner, McNamara, & Chien (2012).

FIGURE 10

By Fifth Grade, More than Three-Fourths of Students Who Began as ELs Demonstrated Proficiency on the ACCESS Test

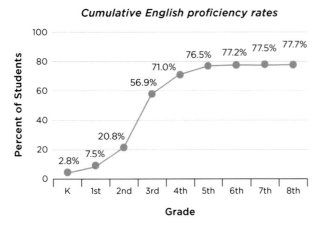

Cumulative English proficiency rates

only 196 (5 percent) went on to demonstrate proficiency by the end of eighth grade. By the end of eighth grade, one in five students who began as ELs in kindergarten—students who were continuously-enrolled in CPS throughout their elementary years, and their schooling was never interrupted by a switch in district—had not yet demonstrated proficiency on the ACCESS test.

Conversely, four in five students who began as ELs had demonstrated proficiency, and were considered former ELs by the end of eighth grade. Although they were not included in any state or district reports about EL outcomes, they made up the majority of students who started as ELs.

Demographics of ELs Who Did and Did Not Reach Proficiency

Of the 18,000 students in our sample who began as ELs, 78 percent demonstrated proficiency by the end of eighth grade, and 22 percent did not. To learn more about which CPS students struggled to attain English proficiency, **Table 3** shows the characteristics of students, based on whether they demonstrated English proficiency by the end of eighth grade, and relative to students who were never classified as ELs.

Compared to other ELs, those ELs who did not demonstrate proficiency by the end of eighth grade were

more likely to be male students and Spanish speakers. They were also slightly more likely to be eligible for free or reduced-price lunch, but both groups of ELs were much more likely to be eligible for free or reduced-price lunch than students who were never classified as ELs. ELs who did not demonstrate proficiency by the end of eighth grade were about as likely to attend CPS preschools as other ELs and students who were never classified as ELs.

ELs who did not demonstrate proficiency were more likely to switch schools than other ELs: 18 percent of ELs who did not demonstrate proficiency attended more than two schools during their K-8 years, compared to 12 percent of ELs who demonstrated proficiency. However, students who were never classified as ELs were the most likely to switch schools: 24 percent attended more than two schools from K-8. Some of the within-district mobility of students never classified as ELs was the result of forced mobility due to the school closings of 2013; however, the differences in mobility between the two groups of ELs were unlikely to be related to the school closings, since both groups were similarly unlikely to attend a school that closed in 2013.

As previously noted, there is some evidence that charter schools may have been less likely to provide mandated bilingual education services during the time when the students in our sample started attending CPS.[65] ELs who did not demonstrate proficiency by eighth grade were not more likely than other ELs to attend charter schools.

Where there were large differences between the two groups of ELs was in their IEP status. ELs who did not demonstrate proficiency were much more likely to have an IEP. In kindergarten, 17 percent of students who did not demonstrate English proficiency by the end of eighth grade already had an IEP, compared to 4 percent of ELs who eventually demonstrated proficiency. This percentage increased steadily over time, such that by the end of eighth grade, more than one-half of students who hadn't demonstrated English proficiency had an IEP, compared to 6 percent of ELs who demonstrated proficiency.

---

65 Belsha (2017, June 28).

TABLE 3

Demographics by English Proficiency Status

	English Learners who Demonstrated Proficiency by Eighth Grade	English Learners who Did Not Demonstrate Proficiency by Eighth Grade	Never Classified as English Learners
Number	14,192	4,072	34,861
Male	49%	60%	50%
Latino	88%	96%	33%
Black	1%	1%	52%
Spanish Speakers	88%	96%	Not Available
Eligible for Free/ Reduced-Price Lunch	93%	97%	82%
Attended CPS Pre-K	64%	63%	66%
Attended More than 2 Schools from K-8	12%	18%	24%
Had an IEP:			
...in Kindergarten	4%	17%	5%
...in Third Grade	5%	32%	10%
...in Eighth Grade	6%	55%	15%
Attended Charter School:			
...in Kindergarten	5%	3%	7%
...in Third Grade	7%	5%	9%
...in Eighth Grade	12%	12%	13%

Recall that in Chapter 1, we saw that as a group, students who began as ELs were no more likely than other students to be identified as needing special education services. This suggests that ELs weren't necessarily more likely to have an IEP, but that ELs who also needed special education services struggled more than their peers to demonstrate proficiency. Of students who began as ELs and also had an IEP, only 26 percent demonstrated proficiency by the end of eighth grade, as opposed to 88 percent of ELs who did not have an IEP.[66] Again, proficiency in English is determined by a student's ability to score well on the ACCESS test. As discussed in Chapter 1, ELs who also have an IEP must meet the same standards and cut scores as other ELs on the ACCESS test to demonstrate proficiency.

Growth on ACCESS among ELs Who Never Achieved Proficiency

Why did some EL students struggle to demonstrate proficiency on the ACCESS test? One possibility is that students were not acquiring English language skills and showing growth on the ACCESS assessment. However, students who did not achieve proficiency in English by the end of eighth grade did show growth on the ACCESS over time that was similar to the growth of students who were proficient in third grade (**see Figure 11**).[67] Recall that additional skills are required at each grade level to demonstrate proficiency on the ACCESS test, such that more is expected from a fourth-grader than a third-grader to meet the proficiency target. Thus, students who did not demonstrate proficiency were

---

66 These figures refer to the IEP status of students who begin as ELs in their expected eighth-grade year. If a student previously had an IEP but was reidentified as no longer needing an IEP, they would not be included.

67 Their growth was larger in kindergarten and smaller from sec-

ond to third grade, compared to students who achieved proficiency in third grade. The lower growth in third grade was likely a selection effect as students who had a good testing day and happened to score higher than the cut-off by chance would be put into the group of students proficient by third grade.

growing in their English skills, but they were not growing enough over time to catch up to the proficiency cutoff.

Instead, as shown in **Figure 11**, ELs who did not demonstrate proficiency by the end of eighth grade began with lower English proficiency levels. Already in kindergarten, students scoring at the 75th percentile of the group that did not demonstrate proficiency by eighth grade scored lower than students scoring at the 50th percentile of ELs who went on to demonstrate proficiency in the third grade. It is difficult to accurately test students in kindergarten, and the kindergarten test is somewhat different than the tests at older grades. The first-grade test is more similar to the tests given at later grade levels; on this test, the middle 50 percent of the two groups did not overlap at all on the ACCESS. That is, the 75th percentile first-grade ACCESS score of the group that did not demonstrate proficiency was lower than the 25th percentile of the group that showed proficiency in third grade. The students who did not go on to demonstrate proficiency by eighth grade started out with lower initial levels of proficiency, and they did not improve enough to catch up with other students. Remember that the scale score required for proficiency

increases as students get older, to correspond with higher expectations at higher grade levels. This means students were showing improved English skills, yet were always remaining below the proficiency cut-off score.

Summary

Of the 18,000 continuously-enrolled students in our sample who began as ELs, more than one-half demonstrated proficiency by the end of third grade, and four out of five demonstrated proficiency by the end of eighth grade. These students became former ELs, and whenever CPS reported on the test scores or graduation rates of ELs, this group was not included.

One out of five students who began as an EL was not proficient by the end of eighth grade, and entered high school as an active EL. Male students, and especially students with an IEP, were less likely to demonstrate proficiency than other students. Students who did not demonstrate proficiency began with lower levels of English proficiency, and while they improved their English skills over time, they never passed the cut-score on the ACCESS that determined proficiency for their grade level.

FIGURE 11

ELs who Did Not Demonstrate Proficiency by Eighth Grade had Lower Initial Proficiency

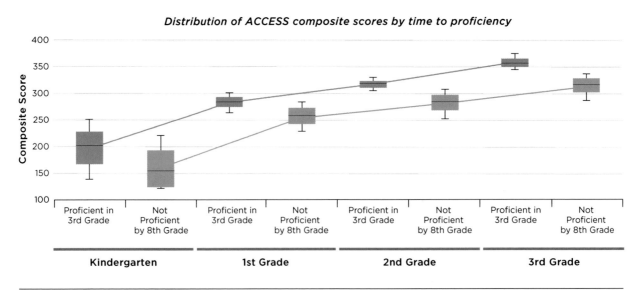

Distribution of ACCESS composite scores by time to proficiency

Note: This graph compares the progress toward English language proficiency on the ACCESS test of two consistent groups—the group of students who demonstrated proficiency in the third grade, and the group of students who did not demonstrate proficiency by eighth grade. Students who demonstrated proficiency in third were chosen as comparison group because they were the largest group of students who began as ELs and had average achievement, relative to the district as a whole. Each box-and-whiskers in this figure displays the distribution of ACCESS scores for a group of students in a particular grade. The horizontal line in the middle of the box shows the median (50th percentile point) of the distribution, i.e. 50 percent of students scored below this score. The top and bottom of the boxes are the 75th and 25th percentile points, respectively. The tops and bottoms of the whiskers show the 90th and 10th percentile points.

CHAPTER 4

Proficient by Eighth Grade? Differing Academic Outcomes

As discussed in the last chapter, most students who began as ELs demonstrated proficiency and became former ELs by the time they reached high school. Twenty-two percent of ELs, however, did not score above the cut score on the ACCESS test by the end of their expected eighth-grade year, and entered high school as active ELs. In order to understand more about these two groups, we examined and compared their academic trajectories in attendance, grades, standardized testing, and Freshman OnTrack status.

Chapter 2 showed these outcomes for all students who began as ELs and provided a promising picture of student performance and growth for the typical EL. However, this method does not highlight those ELs who struggle the most to demonstrate proficiency, who likely need additional support. Separating out academic trajectories based on whether or not an EL demonstrated proficiency by the eighth grade allows us to discover whether ELs who struggle to demonstrate proficiency are also struggling in other academic areas. This method also allows us to learn about the school performance of the larger group of students who begin as ELs and do demonstrate proficiency.

Attendance

Among continuously-enrolled students, both groups of ELs had higher average attendance rates than students who were never classified as ELs, at least in the early grades

In the third grade, ELs who became proficient by eighth grade were absent 3.3 fewer days, and ELs who did not reach proficiency by eighth grade were absent 1.4 fewer days, than students who were never classified as ELs. However, over time, attendance rates declined more for ELs who did not reach proficiency than other students. By the eighth grade, they were absent an average of 0.8 days more than students who were never classified as ELs (see Figure 12).

FIGURE 12

ELs Who Did Not Demonstrate Proficiency by Eighth Grade had Higher Attendance Rates than Students Never Classified as ELs in the Early Grades, but not in the Middle Grades

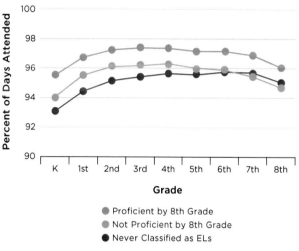

Attendance rates by English proficiency status

- ● Proficient by 8th Grade
- ● Not Proficient by 8th Grade
- ● Never Classified as ELs

Standardized Test Scores

ELs who did not demonstrate English proficiency by eighth grade had much lower scores on both the math and reading NWEA-MAP tests than other continuously-enrolled students, while ELs who demonstrated proficiency had strong performance on these tests. As in Chapter 2, we examined the 2010 kindergarten cohort because they had the longest history of taking the NWEA-MAP, but results were similar when including our other two cohorts (**see Appendix B**).

Compared to students who were never classified as ELs, students who demonstrated proficiency had slightly higher scores, and students who did not demonstrate proficiency had much lower scores on the math NWEA-MAP

In the third grade, students who did not go on to demonstrate proficiency scored 33 percentile points below students never classified as ELs, while in the eighth grade, this gap was 39 percentile points (**see Figure 13a**).

The NWEA-MAP math test is typically administered in English, so these students may have struggled on a test in a language they were still learning. It could also be that students who struggled to score well on the ACCESS test also struggled on other standardized tests.

While ELs who did not demonstrate proficiency by eighth grade had lower test scores, on average, than other students, they showed considerable growth over time in their math scores. In fact, their growth was strong, relative to national trends on the NWEA-MAP. For example, in the third grade, they scored on average at the 12th percentile compared to the national average, while in the eighth grade they scored at the 23rd percentile. This 11 percentile-point growth is meaningful and large, even if their average scores were well below the national average. However, students who did not achieve proficiency by eighth grade did show slightly less growth than other CPS students, and the gap between their scores and other CPS students' did not diminish over time. This was because other CPS students showed even more exceptional growth (for more information about the growth of CPS students relative to the national average, see box on p.20).

In contrast, ELs who demonstrated proficiency by the eighth grade had higher average math scores than students who were never classified as ELs. In the third grade, when the majority of EL students became proficient in English, they scored at the 50th percentile, compared to the national average. CPS students who were never classified as ELs scored at the 45th percentile in third grade. Over the elementary years, ELs who achieved proficiency grew very similarly to students who were never classified as ELs. In the eighth grade, they scored 5 percentile points higher than students who were never classified as ELs. Notably, all continuously-enrolled CPS students grew significantly, compared to the national average.

Figure 13b also shows the average gain score of the three groups of students from year to year. ELs who demonstrated proficiency and students who were never classified as ELs had very similar gains each year, meaning that these groups were growing similarly. However, ELs who did not demonstrate proficiency tended to have smaller math gains. In the fourth, fifth, and seventh grades, other students were gaining about 2-3 points more than students who never demonstrated proficiency.

FIGURE 13

ELs Who Did Not Demonstrate Proficiency by Eighth Grade were Growing at a Slower Rate and had Smaller Gains on the Math NWEA-MAP Test than Other Students

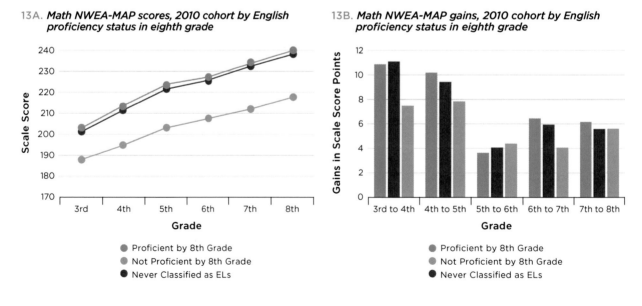

13A. *Math NWEA-MAP scores, 2010 cohort by English proficiency status in eighth grade*

13B. *Math NWEA-MAP gains, 2010 cohort by English proficiency status in eighth grade*

● Proficient by 8th Grade
● Not Proficient by 8th Grade
● Never Classified as ELs

Compared to students who were never classified as ELs, students who demonstrated proficiency had very similar scores, and students who did not demonstrate proficiency had much lower scores on the reading NWEA-MAP test

ELs who did not demonstrate proficiency before high school received lower scores than other continuously-enrolled students on the NWEA-MAP reading test (**see Figure 14a**). The NWEA-MAP reading test is administered in English, so it is not surprising that students would have low scores on a test in a language they are still learning, and for which they have not passed a test of language proficiency. While their reading scores were lower than other students, ELs who did not demonstrate proficiency by eighth grade showed strong growth over time on standardized reading tests, and even grew compared to the national distribution. For example, in the third grade, they scored, on average, at the third percentile compared to the national average, while in the eighth grade they score at the 23rd percentile. Although they were still scoring in the bottom quartile of students in the nation in the eighth grade, this 20 percentile-point growth is meaningful

and large. Their gains were also larger than other CPS students. As shown in **Figure 14b**, in the fifth, sixth, and eighth grades, students who did not demonstrate proficiency were gaining 1-2 points more on the reading test than other students.

ELs who demonstrated proficiency by the eighth grade had very similar average reading scores to students who were never classified as ELs. In the third grade, they scored at the 40th percentile compared to the national average, while students who were never classified as ELs scored at the 42nd percentile. This is particularly notable as most of the ELs who became proficient before high school would have just scored above the ACCESS proficiency cut score in the third-grade year. Over the elementary years, they grew very similarly to students who were never classified as ELs. In the eighth grade, they scored 1 percentile point higher than students who were never classified as ELs. Notably, all continuously-enrolled CPS students grew more compared to the national average, across the three groups.

FIGURE 14

ELs who Never Demonstrated Proficiency Showed Growth and Slightly Larger Gains on the Reading NWEA-MAP Test, but Scored Far Below Other Students

14A. *Reading NWEA-MAP scores, 2010 cohort by English proficiency status in eighth grade*

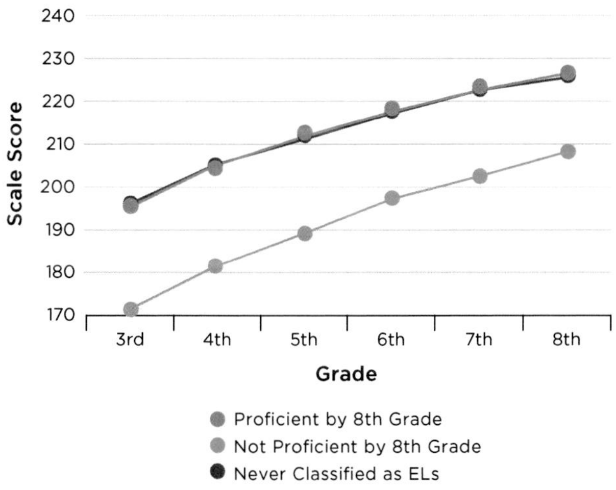

14B. *Reading NWEA-MAP gains, 2010 cohort by English proficiency status in eighth grade*

- Proficient by 8th Grade
- Not Proficient by 8th Grade
- Never Classified as ELs

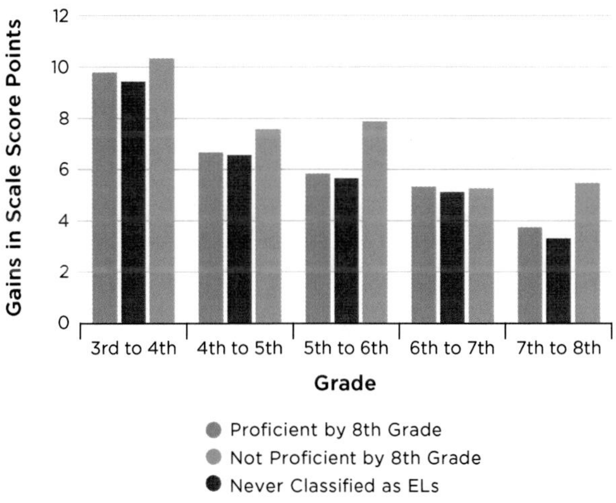

Course Grades (GPA)

As with standardized test scores, students who did not reach proficiency by the end of eighth grade had much lower GPAs, and students who did reach proficiency had slightly higher GPAs, than students who were never classified as ELs

ELs who did not reach proficiency by the end of eighth grade received lower grades in core subjects than other students (**see Figure 15**). In the second grade, their average core GPA was 2.18, or about a C+, compared to an average of 2.95, or about a B, for students who were never classified as ELs. ELs who did not demonstrate proficiency showed larger improvements in their core GPAs by the end of their elementary careers—by the eighth grade, their average core GPA was a 2.51. As mentioned in Chapter 2, this growth in GPA likely indicates increasing skills and competencies gained by active ELs over the years, but also might be influenced by a CPS policy enacted in 2016 which decreed that ELs could not be allowed to fail a course solely due to their lack of English proficiency.

ELs who demonstrated proficiency by the end of eighth grade had the highest average core GPAs of the three groups examined. In the second grade, their average core GPA was a 3.07, compared to an average of 2.95, for students who were never classified as ELs.

FIGURE 15

ELs Who Demonstrated Proficiency by Eighth Grade Had the Highest Average Core GPAs

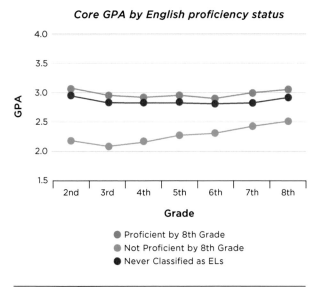

Core GPA by English proficiency status

Note: Students who attended charter schools are not included in this graph.

In the eighth grade, their average core GPA was a 3.05, or about a B, compared to an average of 2.91 for students who were never classified as ELs.

The patterns observed in overall GPA were replicated in course grades for particular subjects; reading and math grades for students who didn't gain proficiency by the end of elementary school were consistently lower than those of the other groups of students, but they improved more over time (**see Figures 16 and 17**). In the third grade, ELs who didn't reach proficiency by the end of eighth grade had average math and reading grades that were about a grade point below those of students who were never classified as ELs (0.8 points lower in math and 1.0 point lower in reading), putting the average grade for this group in the C and C- range for second grade (1.95 in math and 1.67 in reading). By the eighth grade, differences compared to students who were never classified as ELs were smaller, and the average EL who didn't reach proficiency by eighth grade had grades in the C+ range (2.59 in math and 2.37 in reading).

ELs who demonstrated proficiency before high school showed similar patterns in their math and English grades, as observed in their math and English test scores. They received higher grades in math, but similar grades in English, compared to students who were never classified as ELs. In the eighth grade, their average math GPA was a 2.78, or about a B-, compared to an average of 2.59 for students who were never classified as ELs. In the eighth grade, their average reading GPA was a 2.91, or about a B, compared to an average of 2.78 for students who were never classified as ELs.

High School Outcomes

Both groups of ELs were less likely to leave CPS before high school, or be retained in elementary school, than students who were never classified as ELs

As in Chapter 2, **Figure 18** displays high school outcomes only for students in our 2008 and 2009 kindergarten cohorts, given that outcomes for the expected ninth-grade year were not yet available for students in the 2010 cohort.

Only 6 percent of ELs who did not demonstrate proficiency and 7 percent of ELs who demonstrated profi-

FIGURE 16

ELs Who Did Not Reach Proficiency by Eighth Grade Received Lower Grades in Math Classes, but Improved Significantly over Time

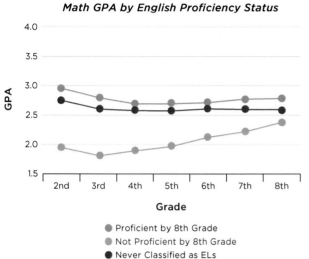

Math GPA by English Proficiency Status

● Proficient by 8th Grade
● Not Proficient by 8th Grade
● Never Classified as ELs

FIGURE 17

ELs Who Did Not Reach Proficiency by Eighth Grade Received Lower GPAs in Reading, but Improved Significantly over the Years

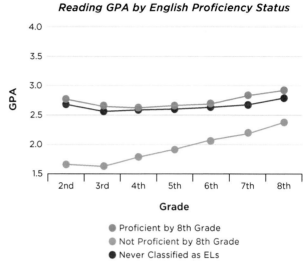

Reading GPA by English Proficiency Status

● Proficient by 8th Grade
● Not Proficient by 8th Grade
● Never Classified as ELs

FIGURE 18

ELs Were Less Likely to Leave CPS or Be Retained, Regardless of Their Proficiency Status

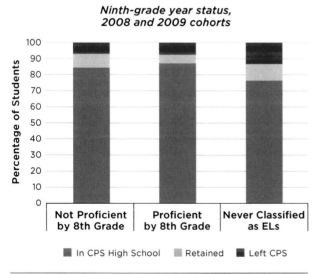

Ninth-grade year status, 2008 and 2009 cohorts

■ In CPS High School   ■ Retained   ■ Left CPS

Note: Data from the year in which students were expected to be in ninth grade.

FIGURE 19

In Ninth Grade, ELs Who Did Not Demonstrate Proficiency by Eighth Grade Were Less Likely to be On-Track to Graduate from High School

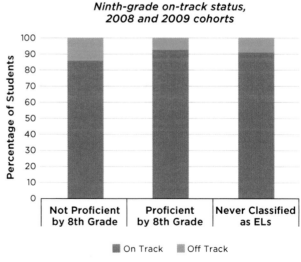

Ninth-grade on-track status, 2008 and 2009 cohorts

■ On Track   ■ Off Track

Note: Conditional on students being in ninth grade, during the year in which they were expected to be in ninth grade.

ciency left CPS before the year they were expected to be in ninth grade, compared to 13 percent of students who were never classified as ELs. Recall that all students in this study were continuously-enrolled in CPS from their kindergarten year to their expected eighth-grade year, but some of these students left CPS for high school.

ELs who did not demonstrate proficiency were more likely to be retained before the ninth grade, compared to ELs who demonstrated proficiency (10 percent vs. 6 percent, respectively). However, 12 percent of students who were never classified as ELs were retained prior to the expected ninth grade year. The relatively low retention rate of students who began as ELs could be due to differences in retention criteria for ELs, as described in Chapter 1.

Among the students who were enrolled in CPS for ninth grade in the expected ninth-grade year (i.e., they had not left the district or been retained), students who did not demonstrate proficiency and entered ninth grade as active ELs were less likely to be considered on-track to graduate than other students; 85 percent were classified as on-track (**see Figure 19 on p.33**). Students who were never classified as ELs and students who demonstrated English proficiency had very similar Freshman OnTrack rates (91 percent and 92 percent, respectively). Previous Consortium work has shown the Freshman OnTrack measure to be highly predictive of on-time high school graduation,[68] so these lower Freshman OnTrack rates are concerning for the long-term outcomes of students who do not reach proficiency.

Summary

The 22 percent of students who began as ELs and did not demonstrate proficiency had high attendance in kindergarten, relative to students never classified as ELs, but their attendance declined over time, and they had lower attendance than other students by the eighth grade. Despite having higher attendance than students never classified ELs in the early grades, students who did not reach proficiency by eighth grade had much lower grades and test scores than other students in English, math, and all of their core courses. They showed growth in test scores and English proficiency that is on-par with other students, or higher, but because they started out with substantially lower test scores, they continued scoring lower. They also improved substantially in their grades over the course of their K-8 years, although this could be influenced by changing CPS grading policies for ELs. They were more likely to be retained than other ELs, although still less likely to be retained than students who were never classified as ELs. When they reached high school, they were less likely to be identified as on-track to graduate. Importantly, this group was small compared to the cohort of students that began as ELs, but they seemed to struggle in school, and could likely have benefited from additional academic support.

The 78 percent of students who began as ELs and demonstrated proficiency on the ACCESS test showed strong performance on school outcomes like attendance, standardized testing, grades, and Freshman OnTrack rates. In all of these outcomes, their performance was similar to or higher than students who were never classified as ELs.

---

68 Easton & Allensworth (2005).

CHAPTER 5

Interpretive Summary

Students who entered CPS schools as ELs had similar, and sometimes higher, academic achievement on multiple measures compared to students who did not start school classified as ELs in the three cohorts we studied. Despite the fact that they were more likely to be economically disadvantaged than other students, their school attendance was higher, and their grades and test scores were similar to students who did not begin school as ELs. They were less likely to be retained than other students, and they were about as likely as students who were never classified as ELs to be considered on-track to graduate high school on time. Their test scores were growing at rates that surpassed the national average.

It is rare to see positive reports of EL outcomes because reporting typically only includes active ELs—students who by the end of elementary school represent only a small percentage of the students who began as ELs. While focusing on active ELs shines a spotlight on students who need the most support, doing so contributes to a misleading narrative about the academic achievement and trajectories of ELs overall.

Supplementing current reporting on ELs with additional sub-groups and metrics would give families, practitioners, and policymakers a more complete understanding of how well schools and districts are supporting active and former ELs

Reporting on the academic achievement of active ELs allows educators to identify students who are underperforming compared to their non-EL peers and therefore likely require additional supports to develop their English skills and succeed in academic settings. However, statistics that only include active ELs provide no information about students who reached the goals that districts have for them by attaining English proficiency—which is the majority of students who start out as ELs.

By excluding students who have successfully reached proficiency, commonly reported metrics give the impression that ELs are not making progress as they move through grade levels. However, in Chicago, their performance was similar—or higher—than the performance of students who did not begin school as ELs. Additionally, highlighting the strong academic outcomes of students who were once classified as ELs but demonstrated proficiency before reaching high school provides a good indication of the effectiveness of the EL services and of schools serving ELs. For families deciding where to enroll their child, and for leaders targeting schools for interventions and support, it is vitally important to know how well individual schools and districts are serving ELs. But with the current metrics, those schools that are most successful at teaching ELs could look just the same, or worse, than schools where students show little growth.

EL performance is contributing to the strong academic growth in CPS

ELs are mastering the same academic skills as other students while learning and becoming proficient in English at the same time. The strong academic growth of ELs in Chicago is particularly notable because CPS students as a whole have shown large academic gains on tests.[69] As one-third of CPS students, ELs are part of this significant growth. Contrary to the story that most publicly available metrics tell, these data show that most students who begin in CPS as ELs are not being

---

69 Reardon & Hinze-Pifer (2017).

left behind, and are instead learning and growing significantly throughout their elementary years. And increasingly, students are being encouraged to aim for the State Seal of Biliteracy, so their proficiency in multiple languages is also being recognized and celebrated.

Support in home language may promote EL academic growth

Unlike states that prioritize English-only education, Illinois policy requires the use of either transitional bilingual programs or dual language programs if there are sufficient students to offer these programs. Research suggests that EL education that includes instruction in students' native languages, like the program models offered in CPS, may be more effective at supporting success for ELs than English-only education.[70] It is possible that the strong academic growth of ELs in Chicago is partly a result of the emphasis in the district on bilingual and dual language programs, rather than English-only education. These programs build on the strengths of students' home language and culture, rather than seeing them as impediments. The Seal of Biliteracy further recognizes the value of building students' skills in multiple languages. However, some ELs do not receive the level of EL services mandated by law; past audits have shown that many CPS schools are not in full compliance with state requirements, and some parents refuse EL services for their children. It is possible that if ELs received more robust services, we may see even stronger growth.

Practitioners could use data, as early as in first grade, to identify ELs who may struggle to reach proficiency and may need additional supports

While many of the ELs in this study were showing typical growth on tests of academic performance compared to other CPS students, about one in five students who began as ELs did not attain proficiency by the end of eighth grade. These students were continuously-enrolled in school from kindergarten to eighth grade. They were learning English at rates that were comparable to other ELs, and they were showing typical growth on other standardized tests. However, the cut points for proficiency on the ACCESS test remained beyond their reach at every grade level. Over one-half had identified disabilities. Issues with learning disabilities may have compounded with issues of learning a language. Some students may simply perform poorly on tests, yet proficiency is determined only by a test. There are also issues with proficiency cut scores changing over time and across grades, as expectations changed and students' designations as English-proficient were affected.

We do not know the implications for students who consistently score below proficiency levels on the ACCESS test. These students retain the label of "ELs" and should continue to receive EL services from their school, which is likely beneficial to their academic experience. However, being unable to demonstrate proficiency in academic English may be a discouraging experience for students, both in terms of their academic self-confidence and how teachers and classmates perceive them.

We know that these ELs in our analyses struggled the most with tests of academic English, and we saw this same group also showed very low performance on the NWEA-MAP assessments. This group of students may not have sufficient academic and language supports. Given the large differences in students' first-grade ACCESS scores between ELs who reached proficiency before high school and those who did not, future research could develop a method of identifying this group of students early on, so that educators could design and implement more effective supports. Students who did not demonstrate English proficiency by the eighth grade showed declining attendance across the middle grade years and a lower likelihood of being on-track for graduation when they entered high school; thus, early targeted support by educators could have a significant positive impact on their later outcomes.

---

70 Collier & Thomas (2012); Umansky & Reardon (2014); Valentino & Reardon (2015).

Student growth in assessments may work for accountability purposes for ELs

Across the nation, growth measures have been widely adopted as key academic indicators under the Every Student Succeeds Act (ESSA). These measures consider the progress made by students at different levels of performance and hold schools accountable based on students' improvements over time, instead of on their performance at a specific point in time. Illinois' accountability system includes students' growth in reading and math test scores as one of its academic indicators.[71] Within CPS, students' attainment and growth in NWEA-MAP test scores are considered as part of the School Quality Ratings Policy metrics for measuring the annual school performance.[72]

We might be concerned that growth on standardized assessments would be very different for ELs than for other students, since they are learning English language at the same time they are learning other academic skills. That would mean we would not expect schools with different percentages of EL students to reach similar student gains on tests, and therefore should not make comparisons between them. However, students who began as ELs showed similar test score gains as their never classified EL peers, both in math and reading. The similarity of students' academic growth trajectories provides some confidence in the use of gains, rather than average scores, to compare performance metrics across schools regardless of the share of their students who are ELs.

Conclusion

Having a clear understanding of the school experiences of non-native English speakers is essential in a district where one-third of students enter without sufficient knowledge of English to fully participate in their classes. Contrary to the story that most publicly available metrics tell, these findings show that most students who begin in CPS as ELs are not being left behind. In fact, many ELs are mastering the same academic skills as other students while learning and becoming proficient in English at the same time. As one-third of the district, ELs have been part of the significant growth that CPS has been showing on standardized tests. At the same time, we have also identified a group of students who, despite being continuously-enrolled in the district since kindergarten, were not able to reach English proficiency by the end of eighth grade, whose academic achievement on multiple measures was lower than their former-EL and non-EL peers, and who likely needed additional supports that they did not receive. Clearly there are still many questions to answer about how ELs experience different types of schools and programs, ELs' experiences through high school, and the experiences of students who enter the district as ELs after kindergarten. Addressing these questions in further studies will be critical to providing adequate support for all students to succeed academically and sustaining their progress in the future.

---

71 Illinois State Board of Education (n.d.).
72 Chicago Public Schools. School quality rating policy (n.d.).

References

Alanís, J. (2010)
The Harrison High School walkouts of 1968: Struggle for equal schools and Chicanismo in Chicago. (Unpublished doctoral dissertation). University of Illinois at Urbana-Champaign, Urbana, IL.

Allensworth, E.M., & Easton, J.Q. (2005)
The on-track indicator as a predictor of high school graduation. Chicago, IL: University of Chicago Consortium on Chicago School Research.

Allensworth, E.M., & Easton, J.Q. (2007)
What matters for staying on-track and graduating in Chicago Public High Schools: A close look at course grades, failures, and attendance in the freshman year. Chicago, IL: University of Chicago Consortium on Chicago School Research.

Allensworth, E.M. Gwynne, J.A., Moore, P., & de la Torre, M. (2014)
Looking forward to high school and college: Middle grade indicators of readiness in Chicago Public Schools. Chicago, IL: University of Chicago Consortium on Chicago School Research.

Balfanz, R., & Byrnes, V. (2012)
Chronic absenteeism: Summarizing what we know from nationally available data. Baltimore, MD: Johns Hopkins University Center for Social Organization of Schools.

Belsha, K. (2017, June 28)
English learners often go without required help at Chicago schools. *Chicago Reporter.* Retrieved from https://www.chicagoreporter.com/english-learners-often-go-without-required-help-at-chicago-schools/

Buck, C.D. (1903)
A sketch of the linguistic conditions of Chicago. Chicago, IL: The University of Chicago Press.

Chang, H.N., & Romero, M. (2008)
Present, engaged and accounted for: The critical importance of addressing chronic absence in the early grades. New York, NY: National Center for Children in Poverty (NCCP) and the Mailman School of Public Health at Columbia University.

Chicago Public Schools. (n.d.)
Language and cultural education. Retrieved from https://cps.edu/Pages/EnglishLearnerPrograms.aspx

Chicago Public Schools. (n.d.)
Language and cultural education: Seal of biliteracy. Retrieved from https://cps.edu/Pages/SealofBiliteracy.aspx

Chicago Public Schools. (n.d.)
School quality rating policy. Retrieved from https://cps.edu/Performance/Pages/PerformancePolicy.aspx

Chicago Public Schools. (2018, June 4)
Mayor Emanuel and CPS announce record number of students earn state seal of biliteracy. Retrieved from https://cps.edu/News/Press_releases/Pages/PR1_06_04_18.aspx

Chicago Public Schools Policy Manual. (2009)
Elementary school promotion (Board report 09-1028-PO2). Chicago, IL: Chicago Public Schools.

Collier, V.P. & Thomas, W.P. (2012)
The astounding effectiveness of dual language education for all. *NABE Journal of Research and Practice, 2*(1), 1-20.

Colorin Colorado. (n.d.)
Disproportionate representation of culturally and linguistically diverse students in special education: Measuring the problem. Retrieved from http://www.colorincolorado.org/article/disproportionate-representation-culturally-and-linguistically-diverse-students-special

Conger, D. (2009)
Testing, time limits, and English Learners: Does age of school entry affect how quickly students can learn English? *Social Science Research, 38*(2), 383-396.

Ehrlich, S.B., Gwynne, J.A., Pareja, A.S., Allensworth, E.M., Moore, P., Jagesic, S., & Sorice, E. (2014)
Preschool attendance in Chicago Public Schools: Relationships with learning outcomes and reasons for absences. Chicago, IL: University of Chicago Consortium on Chicago School Research.

Gottfried, M.A. (2010)
Evaluating the relationship between student attendance and achievement in urban elementary and middle schools: An instrumental variables approach. *American Educational Research Journal, 47*(2), 434-465.

Greenberg Motamedi, J., Singh, M., & Thompson, K.D. (2016)
English learner student characteristics and time to reclassification: An example from Washington state (REL 2016-128). Washington, DC: U.S. Department of Education, Institute of Education Sciences, National Center for Education Evaluation and Regional Assistance, Regional Educational Laboratory Northwest.

Gwynne, J.A., Pareja, A.S., Ehrlich, S.B., & Allensworth, E.M. (2012)
What matters for staying on-track and graduating in Chicago Public Schools: A focus on English Language Learners. Chicago, IL: University of Chicago Consortium on Chicago School Research.

Hakuta, K., Butler, Y.G., & Witt, D. (2000)
How long does it take English learners to attain proficiency? (University of California Linguistic Minority Research Institute Policy Report 2000-1). Santa Barbara, CA: University of California-Santa Barbara.

Halle, T., Hair, E., Wandner, L., McNamara, M., & Chien, N. (2012)
Predictors and outcomes of early vs. later English language proficiency among English language learners. *Early Childhood Research Quarterly, 27*(1), 1-20.

Herrick, M.J. (1971)
The Chicago schools: A social and political history. Beverly Hills, CA: Sage Publications.

Hopkins, M., Thompson, K., Linquanti, R., Hakuta, K., & August, D. (2013)
Fully accounting for English learner performance: A key issue in ESEA reauthorization. *Educational Researcher, 42*(2), 101-108.

Illinois Admin. Code tit. 23, § 228.10. (2017)
Transitional bilingual education. Retrieved from https://www.isbe.net/Documents/228ARK.pdf

Illinois Report Card 2017-2018. (n.d.)
PARCC Assessment. Retrieved from https://www.illinois reportcard.com/state.aspx?source=trends&source2=parcc. details&Stateid=IL

Illinois State Board of Education. (n.d.)
State template for the consolidated state plan under the Every Student Succeeds Act. Retrieved from https://www. isbe.net/Documents/ESSAstatePlanforIllinois.pdf

Illinois State Board of Education. (2018a)
City of Chicago SD 299 Report Card. Retrieved from http://webprod.isbe.net/ereportcard/publicsite/getReport. aspx?year=2018&code=150162990_e.pdf

Illinois State Board of Education. (2018b)
Illinois state seal of biliteracy. Retrieved from https://www. isbe.net/Documents/Seal-Biliteracy-Report-SY18.pdf

Johnson, J.S., & Newport, E.L. (1989)
Critical period effects in second language learning: The influence of maturational state on the acquisition of English as a second language. *Cognitive Psychology, 21*(1), 60-99.

Lin, J. & Neild, R.C. (2017)
Finding their stride: Kindergarten English learners and time to proficiency in the School District of Philadelphia. Philadelphia, PA: Philadelphia Education Research Consortium.

Mid-Atlantic Equity Consortium. (2016)
English learners & disproportionality in special education. Retrieved from https://maec.org/wp-content/uploads/ 2016/04/English-Learners-and-Disproportionality-in-Special-Ed.pdf

National Assessment of Educational Progress. (2017)
National student group scores and score gaps. Retrieved from https://www.nationsreportcard.gov/math_2017/ nation/gaps?grade=4

National Center for Education Statistics. (n.d.)
The condition of education at a glance. Retrieved from https://nces.ed.gov/programs/coe/ataglance.asp

Paral, R. (2003)
Chicago's immigrants break old patterns. Washington, DC: Migration Policy Institute. Retrieved from https://www. migrationpolicy.org/article/chicagos-immigrants-break-old-patterns

Reardon, S.F., & Hinze-Pifer, R. (2017)
Test score growth among Chicago Public School students, 2009-2014. Palo Alto, CA: Stanford Center for Education Policy Analysis.

Romero, M., & Lee, Y. (2007)
A national portrait of chronic absenteeism in the early grades. New York, NY: National Center for Children in Poverty.

Rumberger, R.W. (2015)
Student mobility: Causes, consequences, and solutions. Boulder, CO: National Education Policy Center.

Valentino, R.A., & Reardon, S.F. (2015)
Effectiveness of four instructional programs designed to serve English learners: Variation by ethnicity and initial English proficiency. *Educational Evaluation and Policy Analysis, 37*(4), 612-637.

Umansky, I.M., & Reardon, S.F. (2014)
Reclassification patterns among Latino English learner students in bilingual, dual immersion, and English immersion classrooms. *American Educational Research Journal, 51*(5), 879-912.

United States of America v. Board of Education of the City of Chicago. (1980).
No 80 C 5124, Document 1251. Retrieved from https://www.chicagoreporter.com/wp-content/ uploads/2017/06/0_Consent-Decree-1980.pdf

United States of America v. Board of Education of the City of Chicago. (2009)
No 80 CV 5124, Document 1336. Retrieved from https:// www.justice.gov/sites/default/files/crt/legacy/2010/12/14/ cpsbrief.pdf

U.S. Department of Education. (n.d.)
Academic performance and outcomes for English Learners. Retrieved from https://www2.ed.gov/datastory/el-out-comes/index.html

Appendix A
Data and Sample

Data

Data for the analysis come from CPS administrative records, including information on demographics, school enrollment, high school outcomes, and test scores. All of these data sources are linked together using a unique student identifier.

Sample

Our study followed 53,125 students among three cohorts of first-time kindergartners (they had not been enrolled in kindergarten in CPS in the previous school year) in 2007-08, 2008-09, and 2009-10. Students in our sample were continuously-enrolled from kindergarten through the school year in which they would be expected to reach the eighth grade (2015-16, 2016-17,

TABLE A.1

Description of Variables

Variables	Descriptions
Student Variables	Demographic variables such as gender, race/ethnicity, special education status, free or reduced-price lunch eligibility, attendance to pre-school, attendance to charter school, and home language.
Test Scores	• Student performance on the ACCESS for ELL test. The test measures students' academic English proficiency in four domains: reading, writing, speaking, and listening. ELs take the ACCESS K-12, until they score above the state-determined cut-off and are considered English proficient. Students' ACCESS scores reflect their English proficiency levels ranging from Level 1 (Entering) to Level 6 (Reaching). From each kindergarten cohort, we identified students as ELs based on whether they took the ACCESS test in the spring of the academic year and whether they scored high enough to demonstrate English proficiency. • Student performance on the NWEA-MAP in math and reading in the spring testing window. Students took the NWEA in English. Students' scaled scores are transformed into percentile ranks to describe how well they are performing relative to other students in a nationwide normative sample. Students from the 2010 kindergarten cohort took the test from third to eighth grade. Students from the 2008 and 2009 cohorts were only tested in grades 5-8 and 4-8, respectively.
Grades (Core GPA)	Students' core GPA is the average of final grades earned in the following subjects: math, English, science, and social studies on a 4-point scale where an A=4. Core GPA was computed from second to eighth grade.
Attendance	Percent of days attended is the proportion of the number of days attended (present in school) out of the number of days enrolled. Students who were enrolled for fewer than 110 days were excluded from the sample.
High School Variables	Percent of students enrolled in elementary and high school, and percent of students who left the district in the expected ninth-grade year. Additionally, Freshman OnTrack indicator for students enrolled in ninth grade in the expected year. Ninth-graders are on-track if they earn at least five full-year course credits and have failed no more than one semester in a core course during their first year of high school. These variables are currently unavailable for students in the 2010 kindergarten cohort, since they are expected to reach high school in the 2019 school year.

and 2017-18, respectively). If students were retained in a grade, or skipped a grade, they remained in the sample with their original kindergarten cohort.

We divided our sample into two groups: students who began kindergarten classified as ELs and students who were never classified as ELs, throughout their elementary years. **Table A.2** displays the total number of students in our sample and in each cohort by EL status.

Within the group of ELs, we classified students into two sub-groups based on their English proficiency status: students who scored above the cut-score on the ACCESS test and demonstrated English proficiency by eighth grade and students whose score was not high enough and remained classified as active ELs in the eighth grade. **Table A.3** presents the number of students in each of these EL groups for the three cohorts and the whole sample.

TABLE A.2

Sample Cohort Membership by EL Status

Students Continuously Enrolled in CPS from Kindergarten to Eighth Grade			
	Began as English Learners	Never Classified as English Learners	Overall sample
Number	**18,264**	**34,861**	**53,125**
...from 2008 K Cohort	5,565	10,839	16,404
...from 2009 K Cohort	6,179	12,231	18,410
...from 2010 K Cohort	6,520	11,791	18,311

TABLE A.3

Sample Cohort Membership by English Proficiency Status

Students Continuously Enrolled in CPS from Kindergarten to Eighth Grade			
	English Learners who Demonstrate Proficiency by Eighth Grade	English Learners who Do Not Demonstrate Proficiency by Eighth Grade	Never Classified as English Learners
Number	**14,192**	**4,072**	**34,861**
...from 2008 cohort	4,381	1,184	10,839
...from 2009 cohort	4,808	1,371	12,231
...from 2010 cohort	5,003	1,517	11,791

Appendix B

NWEA-MAP Test Scores in Math and Reading for Students in the 2008 and 2009 Kindergarten Cohorts

In Chapters 2 and 4, we presented NWEA-MAP math and reading test scores only for students in the 2010 kindergarten cohort, since they had the longest history of taking the tests. **Table B.1** displays NWEA-MAP math and reading scores for students in the 2008 and 2009 cohorts, who were only tested in grades 5-8 and 4-8, respectively. As shown in Table B.1, achievement trends were similar for these two younger cohorts. Students who began as ELs were scoring similarly to students never classified as ELs. In reading, students who began as ELs started out having lower scores than their peers, but this difference grew narrower by the end of elementary school.

Similarly, **Table B.2** presents NWEA-MAP math and reading scores for students in the 2008 and 2009 cohorts, divided by their English proficiency status. Students who began kindergarten classified as ELs before demonstrating English proficiency on the ACCESS test by eighth grade scored similarly, or even better, than students who were never classified as ELs. Over time, these students were growing at similar rates in math and reading as their never classified as ELs peers. However, ELs who did not demonstrate proficiency before high school received lower scores than other continuously-enrolled students on the NWEA-MAP tests. While they had lower test scores, on average, than other students, they showed considerable growth over time.

TABLE B.1

Math and Reading NWEA-MAP Scale Scores by EL Status

2008 and 2009 Kindergarten Cohorts					
		Math NWEA-MAP Scale Scores		Reading NWEA-MAP Scale Scores	
Cohort	Grade-Level	Began as ELs	Never Classified as ELs	Began as ELs	Never Classified as ELs
2008	5th	216.6	217.2	205.0	208.1
	6th	221.8	222.8	212.0	214.7
	7th	228.7	229.1	217.5	220.1
	8th	235.0	235.5	222.4	224.9
2009	4th	208.8	210.9	198.7	203.8
	5th	217.4	219.7	206.4	211.4
	6th	222.1	224.7	212.4	216.7
	7th	228.8	231.6	218.0	222.3
	8th	234.5	236.9	222.7	226.5

TABLE B.2

Math and Reading NWEA-MAP Scale Scores by English Proficiency Status

2008 and 2009 Kindergarten Cohorts							
		Math NWEA-MAP Scale Scores			Reading NWEA-MAP Scale Scores		
Cohort	Grade-Level	Proficient by 8th Grade	Not Proficient by 8th Grade	Never Classified as ELs	Proficient by 8th Grade	Not Proficient by 8th Grade	Never Classified as ELs
2008	5th	220.4	200.9	217.2	209.8	185.7	208.1
	6th	225.7	206.2	222.8	216.4	194.6	214.7
	7th	232.9	211.8	229.1	221.7	200.5	220.1
	8th	239.3	217.7	235.5	226.3	206.6	224.9
2009	4th	212.3	195.2	210.9	203.6	178.9	203.8
	5th	221.5	201.7	219.7	211.2	188.0	211.4
	6th	226.2	206.7	224.7	216.8	195.6	216.7
	7th	233.1	212.2	231.6	222.2	201.8	222.3
	8th	239.1	216.9	236.9	226.7	207.3	226.5

ABOUT THE AUTHORS

MARISA de la TORRE is a Senior Research Associate and Managing Director at the University of Chicago Consortium on School Research. Her research interests include urban school reform, school choice, early indicators of school success, and English Learners. Before joining UChicago Consortium, Marisa worked for the Chicago Public Schools in the Office of Research, Evaluation, and Accountability. She received a master's degree in economics from Northwestern University.

ALYSSA BLANCHARD is a Research Analyst at the UChicago Consortium on School Research. Her current research focuses on the academic experiences of English Learners and non-cognitive predictors of student success. Previously, she worked as a Graduate Assistant at the Tennessee Education Research Alliance. She received an MPP in Educational Policy and a BA in Public Policy from Vanderbilt University.

ELAINE M. ALLENSWORTH is the Lewis-Sebring Director of the UChicago Consortium on School Research, where she has conducted research on educational policy and practice for the last 20 years. She works with policymakers and practitioners to bridge research and practice, providing advice to researchers across the country about conducting research-practice partnerships, and serving on panels, policy commissions, and working groups at the local, state and national levels. She holds a PhD in Sociology from Michigan State University and was once a high school Spanish and science teacher.

SILVANA FREIRE is a Research Analyst at the UChicago Consortium on School Research. In this role, she conducts quantitative research to learn more about the experiences of CPS students and to identify relevant factors that play a key role in students' academic success and equitable learning opportunities. Before joining the UChicago Consortium, Silvana worked as a Research Assistant at the Graduate School of Education at Stanford University, while she was getting her MA degree in International Education Policy Analysis.

UCHICAGO Consortium
on School Research

1313 East 60th Street
Chicago, Illinois 60637

T 773.702.3364
F 773.702.2010

@UChiConsortium
consortium.uchicago.edu

OUR MISSION The University of Chicago Consortium on School Research (UChicago Consortium) conducts research of high technical quality that can inform and assess policy and practice in the Chicago Public Schools. We seek to expand communication among researchers, policymakers, and practitioners as we support the search for solutions to the problems of school reform. The UChicago Consortium encourages the use of research in policy action and improvement of practice, but does not argue for particular policies or programs. Rather, we help to build capacity for school reform by identifying what matters for student success and school improvement, creating critical indicators to chart progress, and conducting theory-driven evaluation to identify how programs and policies are working.

THE UNIVERSITY OF CHICAGO

UEI URBAN EDUCATION INSTITUTE

ISBN 978-0-9995509-6-0

9 780999 550960

Made in the USA
Monee, IL
17 October 2020